CHECK YOUR ENGLISH VOCABULARY FOR

LAW

by

Rawdon Wyatt

BLOOMSBURY INFORMATION

LONDON · NEW YORK · OXFORD · NEW DELHI · SYDNEY

BLOOMSBURY INFORMATION
Bloomsbury Publishing Plc
50 Bedford Square, London, WC1B 3DP, UK
29 Earlsfort Terrace, Dublin 2, Ireland

BLOOMSBURY, BLOOMSBURY INFORMATION and the Diana logo
are trademarks of Bloomsbury Publishing Plc

First published 1996 by Peter Collin Publishing
Second edition published 1998 by Bloomsbury Publishing Plc
Third edition published 2006
Reprinted by Bloomsbury Academic 2012, 2016, 2017, 2018 (twice), 2022

A catalogue record for this book is available from the British Library.

A catalog record for this book is available from the Library of Congress.

ISBN: PB: 978-1-3994-0564-5
eBook: 978-1-4081-0239-8

Series: Check Your Vocabulary

Typeset by Saxon Graphics Ltd, Derby
Printed and bound in Great Britain

To find out more about our authors and books visit
www.bloomsbury.com and sign up for our newsletters.

Introduction

This book has been written for anyone working or training to work in the legal profession, or for anyone whose job requires them to have a working knowledge of legal words and terms. The various exercises throughout the book focus on the key vocabulary that you might be expected to understand and use on a day-to-day basis.

You should not go through the exercises in this book mechanically. It is better to choose areas that you are unfamiliar with, or areas that you feel are of specific interest or importance to yourself.

Each exercise is accompanied by a full answer key at the back of the book. This key also gives you other information about particular vocabulary items (for example, words with similar meanings, alternative words and expressions, etc) that are not covered in the exercises themselves.

When you are doing the exercises, there are a few important points you should consider:

1. Many of the words, expressions and accompanying notes are based primarily on the English and Welsh legal system. However, there are also many 'generic' words which can be applied across the international legal spectrum, and would be recognised in other places such as the USA and Canada.

2. Not all of the vocabulary practised in this book is legal vocabulary *per se* (see page 45 to find out what this expression means), but would be used in a legal context (for example, at a trial or tribunal, or when producing a contract or negotiating business terms).

3. A lot of the words and expressions which have been presented here in a particular context (for example, words connected with a criminal law procedure) might also 'cross over' into other areas of law. A jury, for example, is usually employed at a criminal trial, but might also be used in some civil cases, such as libel.

It is very important to keep a record of new words and expressions that you learn. On page 64 of this book, you will find a vocabulary record sheet which you can photocopy as many times as you like and use to build up a 'bank' of useful words and expressions. It is accompanied on the following page by a sample sheet that shows you how to record a particular vocabulary item. Keep your record sheets in a file or folder and review them on a regular basis so that the words and expressions become an 'active' part of your legal vocabulary.

We recommend that you keep a good dictionary with you, and refer to it when necessary. Many of the words and expressions in this book (together with their definitions) can be found in the *A & C Dictionary of Law*. For general vocabulary reference, the *Macmillan English Dictionary* is also an excellent resource.

No vocabulary book can possibly contain all of the legal words and expressions that you are likely to come across or need, so it is important you acquire new vocabulary from other sources. On the next page you will find a short list of useful sources that were consulted during the writing of this book, and you should also read as much as possible from a variety of other sources, including journals, papers and case reports (many of which are available on the Internet).

Contents

The following websites were a useful reference source during the writing of this book, and are recommended if you want to develop your legal vocabulary further, or if you want to learn more about laws, legal systems, etc, (especially those in the United Kingdom).

www.informationcommissioner.gov.uk
www.family-solicitors.co.uk
www.interactive-law.co.uk
www.law.ed.ac.uk
www.citizensadvice.org.uk
www.uklegal.com
www.compactlaw.co.uk
www.lawontheweb.co.uk
www.legalservices.gov.uk
www.media-solicitors.co.uk
www.unhchr.ch (very useful if you want to know more about the United Nations and human rights)
www.bench-marks.org (an excellent website if you want to know more about the underlying principles of corporate governance and responsibility)

For reference see *Dictionary of Law* 4th edition (A & C Black 0-7475-6636-4).

Before you begin: Essential words

The words in this exercise are used a lot in the legal profession, and appear at various stages throughout this book, so it is important you understand what they mean before you do any of the other exercises. Match the definitions on the left with the words on the right. Note that (a) there are more words than definitions, and (b) many of the words on the right can have more than one meaning, but only one of those meanings is in the column on the left. Note that many of the words and accompanying expressions in this exercise (and in the following exercises on business law) are not exclusive to business law, but may also be applied to other legal and general areas.

Definitions	Words
1. Money claimed by someone as compensation for harm done.	appeal
2. To send someone to prison or to a court.	arrest
3. An adjective referring to a judge or to the law.	binding
4. Not guilty of a crime.	breach
5. Any act which is not legal.	case
6. A person who has studied law and can act for people on legal business.	charge
7. A disagreement or argument between parties.	civil
8. A specialist court outside the judicial system which examines special problems.	claimant
9. A set of arguments or facts put forward by one side in a legal proceeding.	commit
10. An official who presides over a court.	contract
11. To make an allegation in legal proceedings.	convict
12. Someone who is accused of a crime in a criminal case.	court
13. A person who makes a claim against someone in a civil court.	crime
14. An agreement reached after an argument.	criminal
15. To hold someone legally so as to charge them with a crime.	damages
16. A case which is being heard by a committee, tribunal or court of law.	defence
17. To find that someone is guilty of a crime.	defendant
18. Failure to carry out the terms of an agreement.	dispute
19. To bring someone to court to answer a criminal charge.	evidence
20. To ask a high law court to change its decision or sentence.	fine
21. To say that someone has committed a crime.	guilty
22. Having the legal ability to force someone to do something.	hearing
23. An adjective referring to the rights and duties of private persons or organisations.	injunction
24. The arguments used when fighting a case.	innocent
25. A legal agreement between two or more parties.	judge
26. An adjective referring to crime.	judicial
27. A group of 12 citizens who decide whether or not someone is guilty in a trial.	jury
28. A written or spoken statement of facts which helps to prove or disprove something at a trial.	lawyer
29. To order someone to pay money as a punishment.	legal
30. A court order telling someone to stop doing something, or not to do something.	offence
	plead
	prosecute
	sentence
	settlement
	trial
	tribunal

1

For reference see *Dictionary of Law* 4th edition (A & C Black 0-7475-6636-4).

Business law 1: Key adjectives

Exercise 1: Look at these sentences and decide if the word in bold is being used correctly in the context of the sentence (there is an *explanation* of the word that should be used in brackets at the end of the sentence). If you think the word is wrong, look for the correct word. You will find this in one of the other sentences.

1. When pieces of broken glass were found in some of its food products, the company was held **eligible**. (*responsible for what had happened*)

2. When he was asked to explain his actions, he had no **valid** explanations. (*being acceptable because it is true or relevant*)

3. The sacked workers claimed unfair dismissal, and demanded a fair and **intangible** hearing. (*not biased or prejudiced*)

4. Goodwill is one of a company's **admissible** assets, and as such it cannot be declared as part of the company's capital. (*difficult to value as it does not exist physically*)

5. He was accused of trying to obtain a **fiduciary** advantage by getting involved in insider dealing. (*financial*)

6. At the trial, the judge took the **unprecedented** step of asking the claimant to remove his shirt. (*not having happened before*)

7. The company solicitor examined the contract very carefully, and eventually declared it **irreconcilable**. (not having any legal effect)

8. The documents produced were not considered relevant to the case and were therefore not **unanimous**. (*referring to evidence which a court will allow to be used*)

9. The magazine was acquitted of libel when the jury returned a **gross** verdict of 'not guilty'. (*where everyone votes in the same way*)

10. All shareholders are **accountable** to vote at the Annual General Meeting. (*able or allowed to do something*)

11. The judge accepted that Mr Johnson could not go back to work in the same company because of **void** differences of opinion between him and the Directors. (*very strong, so that it is not possible for two sides to reach an agreement*)

12. The rail company was accused of **impartial** negligence by failing to ensure passengers' safety. (*serious*)

13. Interest charges are tax **deductible** so we haven't made as much as we had hoped. (*able to be removed*)

14. After a terrible year, during which it lost almost £8 million, the company was declared **insolvent**. (*not able to pay debts*)

15. A company director has a **pecuniary** duty to the company he works for and the people who work there. (*acting as trustee for someone else, or being in a position of trust*)

For reference see *Dictionary of Law* 4th edition (A & C Black 0-7475-6636-4).

Exercise 2: In this exercise, the first part of each word is already in the sentence. Complete it with the second part, which you will find in the box.

__atim •	__ditional •	__dulent •	__empt •	___ended •	__erial
__gious •	__inal •	__itual •	__ndant •	__orate •	__pational
	__sible •	__tiable •	__tory •	__vent	

1. Because of the recent phenomenon of the 'compensation culture', claims for **occu____** accidents have almost doubled in the last ten years. (*referring to jobs and work*)

2. So many complaints about the company's behaviour were reported that a **manda____** injunction was imposed ordering them to cease trading. (*obligatory or necessary according to the law or rules*)

3. Some special savings accounts are popular with small businesses because the interest paid is **ex____** from tax. (*not required to pay, or not covered by law*)

4. The terms of the contract are **nego____** up to the moment it is signed. (*able to be changed by discussion*)

5. The claimant produced a **verb____** transcript of the conversation he had had with the defendant. (*in the exact words*)

6. On the claimant's application for summary judgement, the defendant was given **uncon____** leave to defend himself. (*with no conditions attached*)

7. The company was accused of making a **frau____** insurance claim by exaggerating the value of the goods it had lost. (*not honest, aiming to deceive people for financial gain*)

8. Technically we can sue the company for breach of contract, although this is not really a **fea____** option. (*possible or practical*)

9. New legislation has made Clause 6b of the contract **redu____**. (*no longer needed or valid*)

10. **Hab____** breaches of safety regulations are being investigated by the Health and Safety Officer. (*doing something repeatedly*)

11. When he bought the company, it was barely **sol____** but he turned it into one of the most successful organisations in the country. (*having enough money to pay debts*)

12. The lawsuit against the organisation was dropped because there was not enough **mat____** evidence. (*important or relevant*)

13. We were expecting to receive a big fine, but in the event we were ordered to pay only **nom____** damages. (*a very small amount*)

14. The issues of **corp____** responsibility at local, national and international levels have been receiving a lot of coverage in the press. (*referring to a company*)

15. The contract is **open-____** although there is an initial probationary period. (*with no fixed period, or with some items not specified*)

16. Be careful what you say: some companies are extremely **liti____**. (*very willing to bring a lawsuit against someone to settle a disagreement*)

For reference see *Dictionary of Law* 4th edition (A & C Black 0-7475-6636-4).

Business law 2: Key nouns

Look at the dictionary definitions below, decide what each one is describing, then write your answers in the table on the next page. The first and last letters of each word have already been put into the table for you.

If you complete the table correctly, you will reveal a word in the shaded vertical strip that can be used to complete the sentence in the box at the bottom of the next page.

1. A person who is appointed to deal with financial or other matters on behalf of another person.

2. A licence to trade using a brand name and paying a royalty for it.

3. An official who investigates complaints by the public against government departments or other large organisations (especially banks, travel companies, and electricity, gas, water and telecommunications providers).

4. Somebody who gives a guarantee.

5. A failure to carry out the terms of an agreement, a contract, etc.

6. One of the main conditions of a contract, where one party agrees to what is proposed by the other party. Also the act of signing a bill of exchange to show that you agree to pay for it.

7. The notifiable offence of telling lies when you have made an oath to say what is true in court.

8. Somebody who has committed a civil wrong to somebody, entitling the victim to claim damages.

9. A payment made by a person or company to cover the cost of damage or hardship which he / she / it has caused.

10. An attempt by a third party to make the two sides in an argument agree.

11. A document in which a company acknowledges it owes a debt and gives the company's assets as security.

12. The closing of a company and the selling of its assets.

13. Money claimed by a claimant from a defendant because of harm or damage done, or money awarded by a court to a claimant as a result of harm suffered by the claimant (Clue: this word has already appeared elsewhere in this exercise).

14. The legal responsibility for paying someone for loss or damage incurred.

15. A failure to give proper care to something, especially a duty or responsibility, with the result that a person or property is harmed.

16. The good reputation of a business and its contacts with its customers (for example, the name of the product it sells or its popular appeal to customers).

17. A court order telling a person or a company to stop doing something, or telling them not to do it in the first place.

For reference see *Dictionary of Law* 4th edition (A & C Black 0-7475-6636-4).

#													
1					N						E		
2		F							E				
3		O							N				
4			G							R			
5				B				H					
6		A								E			
7				P					Y				
8		T							R				
9		C								N			
10					M						N		
11			D					E					
12	L							N					
13				D				S					
14	L						Y						
15			N							E			
16				G						L			
17			I							N			

Use the word in the shaded vertical strip to complete this paragraph.

The company promised us that they would send us the goods by March 31st, but since then we have discovered that they knew they couldn't get them to us until the end of May. We lost a lot of money as a result, so we are going to sue them for _____.

Familiarise yourself with the words in this exercise by using them in some of your own sentences. Don't forget to record any new words and expressions you learn (there is a vocabulary record sheet on page 64 which you can photocopy as many times as you like and use to build your own vocabulary 'bank').

For reference see *Dictionary of Law* 4th edition (A & C Black 0-7475-6636-4).

Business law 3: Key verbs

Complete the crossword on page 8 by rearranging the jumbled letters in bold in the sentences below and writing the words and expressions in the appropriate space on the crossword grid. An explanation of each verb is in brackets at the end of each sentence. *Be careful*, as many of the words will need to change their form (for example, to the past simple or past perfect) to fit correctly in the sentence and into the crossword.

<u>Across</u>:

3.   The airline will **dineynifm** passengers for lost luggage to the value of £500. (*to pay for loss or damage suffered*)

4.   The company **ernudketa** to provide quality service at a competitive cost. (*to promise to do something*)

10. The tribunal will **udditecaja** the claim and award damages where necessary. (*to give a judgement between two parties*)

12. In order to raise enough money for its new venture, the company decided to **diqielatu** some of its assets. (*to sell assets or stock to raise cash*)

14. All of our employees are **tielent** to four weeks' holiday a year. (*to have or give someone the right to do something*)

15. A neutral party was called in to **tedaime** between the manager and his staff. (*to try to make two sides in an argument come to an agreement*)

17. The contract is still being **frtad**, but we expect it to be ready for signing early next week. (*to make a first rough plan of a document such as a contract*)

19. A lot of people were unhappy when he was **paintpo** to the post of Managing Director. (*to choose someone for a job*)

20. We must allow sufficient time to **sepela** before we make a claim. (*of time: to pass*)

21. The company has been accused of trying to **efrudad** customers. (*to trick someone so as to obtain money or goods illegally*)

26. The paper has no right to **clodseis** the details of our agreement. (*to tell details*)

28. A court injunction has **nab** the company from trading in the area. (*to forbid something, or make it illegal*)

29. Because a new company has taken over, the contract has been **dvaatineli**. (*to make something no longer valid*)

31. In view of the inconvenience we have caused, we are willing to **vawei** all payments due. (*to say that something is not necessary*)

32. The local authority **gatnr** the company an interest-free loan to start up the new factory. (*to agree to give someone something, or to allow someone to do something*)

For reference see *Dictionary of Law* 4th edition (A & C Black 0-7475-6636-4).

Down:

1. The plan has to be **fatyir** by the board before it can be put into operation. (*to approve officially something that has already been decided*)

2. After he was accused of insider dealing, his firm was **clabstkli** by the government. (*to put goods, people or a company on a list of those that you will not deal with*)

5. Penalties will be applied if you **fdaetul** on your repayments. (*to fail to carry out the terms of a contract, especially to fail to pay back a debt*)

6. When the company was unable to repay the loan, the bank **clefeosor** on its premises. (*to take possession of a property because the owner cannot repay money he / she has borrowed using the property as security*)

7. The case might last longer than we expected, because the defendant is **uditeps** the claim. (*to argue against something; to say that something is not correct*)

8. The judge **dwraa** compensatory damages to the claimant. (*to decide the amount of money to be given to someone*)

9. The company assured us it would do all the work itself, but it **accobnsutrt** part of the job to a local firm. (*to agree with a company that they will do all or part of the work for a project*)

11. The court was unable to decide whether the patent had been **gfriinen**. (*to make a product in the same way as another product which has been patented, and not pay royalties*)

13. The document has been **fcrieyt** as a true copy. (*to make an official declaration in writing*)

16. Non-profit organisations will be **petmex** from tax. (*to free someone from having to pay tax*)

18. The court ordered the company to be **ndwi pu** (2 words). (*to put a company into liquidation*)

19. The claimant **gaelle** that the article was an infringement of his copyright. (*to state, usually in giving evidence, that something has happened or is true*)

22. The company did not **biead yb** (2 words) the terms of the agreement. (*to accept a rule or follow a custom*)

23. On liquidation, the firm's property was **stev** in the bank. (*to transfer to someone the legal ownership and possession of land or a right*)

24. We are **mical** £5,000 as compensation from our suppliers. (*to ask for money*)

25. Mr and Mrs Douglas' solicitor advised them to **ekse** an injunction against the magazine in the High Court. (*to ask for or try to do something*)

27. Workers are allowed to **tkesri** in protest against bad working conditions. (*to stop working because there is no agreement with management*)

30. The company owns several apartments, which it **tel** to private tenants. (*to allow someone to use a building in return for money*)

For reference see *Dictionary of Law* 4th edition (A & C Black 0-7475-6636-4).

8

For reference see *Dictionary of Law* 4th edition (A & C Black 0-7475-6636-4).

Business law 4: Key expressions

Complete definitions 1 – 30 with the first part of an appropriate expression from the first box, and the second part from the second box.

1. An official power giving someone the right to act on someone else's behalf in legal matters is called _____.

2. The protecting of information about individuals stored in a computer from being copied or used wrongly is called _____.

3. _____ is a phrase spoken or written in a letter when attempting to negotiate a settlement which means that the negotiations cannot be referred to in court or relied upon by the other party if discussions fail.

4. A _____ is a business partnership where two or more companies join together as partners for a limited period.

5. _____ is an expression of French origin that is used for something which happens which is out of control of the parties who have signed a contract (for example, a war or a storm), and is also known as an act of God.

6. A _____ refers to the various steps an employee takes if he / she wants to complain about his / her employers.

7. _____ are the contents of a document which regulate the way in which a company's affairs (such as the appointment of directors or the rights of shareholders) are managed.

8. A section in a company's (number 7 above) which requires any shares offered for sale to be first offered to existing shareholders is known as a _____.

9. When a company is put into liquidation, this is often known as _____.

10. The legal responsibility of an employer when employees are subject to accidents due to negligence on the part of an employer is called _____.

11. The legal responsibility of one person for the actions of another person, especially the responsibility of an employer for acts committed by an employee in the course of work, is called _____.

12. A _____ company is a company where each shareholder is responsible for paying the company's debts only to the face value of the shares he / she owns.

For reference see *Dictionary of Law* 4th edition (A & C Black 0-7475-6636-4).

13. A _____ is a legal document setting up a limited company and giving details of its aims, capital structure, and registered office.

14. A _____ is a document showing that a company has repaid a mortgage or charge.

15. A situation where two or more parties share a single legal responsibility, and each party is also liable for the whole claim, is called _____ liability.

16. When a dispute between two parties is settled before it gets to court, it is known as an _____ settlement.

17. When an overseas company (or an individual) cannot access its assets because a court order prevents it from doing so, this is known as a _____.

18. _____ are compensatory payments which are not for a fixed amount of money but are awarded by a court as a matter of discretion depending on the case.

19. The duty to prove that something which has been alleged in court is true is known as the _____.

20. Behaviour which is not suitable for a professional person and goes against the code of practice of a profession is called _____.

21. Facts which are secret and must not be passed on to other people are called _____.

22. A body responsible for hearing work-related complaints as specified by statute is called an _____.

23. An _____ is a legally-binding rule that is imposed on the recipient of private or secret information which states that the recipient should not pass the information on to someone else.

24. The name, design or other feature which identifies a commercial product, has been registered by the maker and cannot be used by other makers is called a 'registered _____'.

25. _____ is something such as a copyright, patent or design which someone has created or produced that no-one else can legally copy, use or sell.

26. The conditions which have to be carried out as part of a contract, or arrangements which have to be made before a contract is valid, are called _____.

27. The removal of someone from a job for a reason that cannot be justified, and which is in breach of contract, is called _____.

28. _____ is an attempt by one company to do better than another company by using methods such as importing foreign products at very low prices or by wrongly criticising a competitor's products.

29. A failure to carry out an essential or basic term of a contract is known as a _____.

30. _____ is when a court orders a company to close and its assets to be sold.

For reference see *Dictionary of Law* 4th edition (A & C Black 0-7475-6636-4).

Consumer rights

Many countries have legislation in place to protect the rights of consumers. In Britain, they are protected by laws such as the *Sale of Goods Act*, the *Supply of Goods and Services Act*, the *Distance Selling Regulations*, the *Consumer Protection Act* and the *Consumer Credit Act*.

Exercise 1: Here is a summary of some of the key points from these laws, and some other information which consumers might find useful. Complete the paragraphs with words and expressions from the box.

```
    1. accurate description    2. as described    3. cooling-off period    4. credit card fraud
         5. credit voucher    6. defective    7. delivery arrangements    8. fit for purpose
    9. give a refund    10. guarantee or warranty    11. opt out of    12. proof of purchase
         13. receipt    14. responsibilities and liabilities    15. satisfactory quality
         16. unsolicited mail    17. unsolicited telemarketing    18. wear and tear
              19. within a reasonable time    20. written confirmation
```

Providers of goods and services (including credit providers and hire companies) all have _____ towards the customer which are aimed at protecting the customer and his / her rights.

When you buy goods, they must be of _____: the condition they are in should match your expectations based on the price you paid. They should also be '_____' (in other words, they must match the description made by the provider and / or the manufacturer), and they must be '_____' (they should do what you expect them to do).

All goods must carry a _____ in case they go wrong or do not meet your expectations.

If you need to return goods a shop or other supplier, you should do so _____: many shops and suppliers specify their own limit, usually 28 days, and can refuse to do anything if there is evidence of unreasonable _____ (signs that the goods have been used more than is normal or for a purpose for which they were not designed).

If you take goods back to a shop, they are entitled to ask for _____, such as a _____, a credit card slip, etc, that shows you actually bought the goods from them.

Many shops may refuse (illegally, if the product you have bought is faulty or _____) to _____, and instead of returning your money will offer you a _____ to use in that shop at a later date.

Where goods or services are ordered on the Internet, on-line shops should offer their customers a _____ after they have ordered them, in case the customer decides to suddenly cancel their order.

On-line shops should give the customer an _____ of the goods being sold, and clearly state the price, _____ and options (how and when the customer can expect to receive their goods, whether there is an extra charge for postage, etc).

On-line shops should also protect customers against _____, and should allow customers to _____ receiving further information and _____, _____ or unsolicited email. They should also send the customer _____ of their order (often in the form of an email sent after the order has been placed).

For reference see *Dictionary of Law* 4th edition (A & C Black 0-7475-6636-4).

> 1. claim for compensation   2. claim form   3. County Court   4. in your favour
> 5. issue the proceedings   6. make a claim   7. poor workmanship   8. preliminary hearing
> 9. reasonable care and skill   10. reasonable charge   11. received satisfaction
> 12. serves the claim   13. Small Claims   14. specified period

If a service is being provided (for example, a mobile phone contract), and there is a _____ for the contract, this must be clearly stated by the provider.

If you buy faulty goods with a credit card, and those goods cost over £100, you have an equal _____ against the seller of the goods and the credit card company.

Where a service such as the repair of a car is being provided, it should be done with _____ (an unsatisfactory standard of work or general _____ should not be accepted by the customer) for a _____ (the customer should not have to pay an excessive amount of money) and within a reasonable time.

If you need to _____ against a shop, company or other provider, because you have not _____ from that shop, company, etc, you can do so through the _____. For claims of less than £5,000 the _____ procedure should be useful.

The process is very simple: after completing a _____, you ask the court to _____. The court then _____ on the company or other provider. Assuming the company responds within the specified time limit, there will be a _____. Later, there will be a main hearing where hopefully the judge will decide _____.

For reference see *Dictionary of Law* 4th edition (A & C Black 0-7475-6636-4).

Exercise 1:

Complete this text, which has been adapted from the A & C Black *Dictionary of Law*, with words or expressions from the box.

```
1. accepted    2. agreement    3. breach    4. consideration    5. contractual liability    6. damages
   7. express    8. implied    9. intention    10. obligations    11. offer    12. reward    13. signed
        14. stated    15. sue    16. terms    17. under seal    18. verbally    19. voided    20. writing
```

A contract can be defined as 'an _____ between two or more parties to create legal _____ between them'. Some contracts are made '_____': in other words, they are _____ and sealed (stamped) by the parties involved. Most contracts are made _____ or in _____. The essential elements of a contract are: (a) that an _____ made by one party should be _____ by the other; (b) _____ (the price in money, goods or some other _____, paid by one party in exchange for another party agreeing to do something); (c) the _____ to create legal relations. The _____ of a contract may be _____ (clearly stated) or _____ (not clearly _____ in the contract, but generally understood). A _____ of contract by one party of their _____ entitles the other party to _____ for _____ or, in some cases, to seek specific performance. In such circumstances, the contract may be _____ (in other words, it becomes invalid).

Exercise 2:

There are many different kinds of contract for different situations. Look at the following paragraphs, and decide what kind of contract is being described or talked about.

1.   I went into the supermarket and chose the items that I wanted. As soon as my basket was full, I headed for the checkout.

2.   My cousin Bob said he was going to get rid of his computer and buy a new one. I said that I needed a computer and suggested I bought his old one. Anyway, we agreed on a price, I gave him a £50 deposit, and agreed to pay the balance in instalments over the next three months. I'm going round to collect the computer this evening.

3.   The property is unfurnished, and the rent is £650 pcm, which has to be paid monthly in arrears. Electricity, gas and phone bills are extra. There's a communal garden and a communal parking area, for which I also have to pay a nominal maintenance fee. The landlord is responsible for any repairs to the property. I'm not allowed to sublet at any time. I've signed the lease for 18 months.

4.   We're opening our own branch in the town centre next week. The deal is fairly simple: we get the right to use the company's name, their trademark, their trade names and products, wear their uniforms and use their stationery. They also provide our staff with all the necessary training, give us invaluable managerial assistance and provide advertising materials. In return, we have to meet specific requirements, such as quality of service, maintaining good customer relations, and following the company's standard procedures. Oh, and buy all the products we sell from them, naturally.

For reference see *Dictionary of Law* 4th edition (A & C Black 0-7475-6636-4).

5.   The total amount you are borrowing is £9,000 at an APR of 6.6%. Repaid in monthly instalments over 3 years, this gives you a monthly repayment figure of £275.46, totalling £9,916.56. You have opted out of the repayment protection premium scheme. If you wish to make an early settlement, the figure above will be recalculated accordingly. As soon as you sign a form, your funds will be released into your bank account. Please note that penalties will be applied if you default on repayments.

6.   This appointment is for a period of two years, following a 4-week probationary period. Your remuneration package includes an annual gross salary of £32,000. You are entitled to sick pay and 6 weeks annual leave after you have been with us for 3 months. Your hours of work are 9 to 5 Monday to Friday, although you may be asked to work overtime during busy periods. The company has its own medical and pension schemes which you may join.

7.   The total cost is £2,870, which is payable in full before the goods can be despatched. Alternatively, we can arrange credit terms, which are interest-free for the first six months. All goods are covered by the manufacturer's warranty, which is valid for one year. If you are not happy with your merchandise, it can be returned for an exchange or full refund (but please note that this is valid for 28 days only, and we will need to see your receipt or other proof of purchase).

8.   A group 7M people carrier is £58 a day. This price includes unlimited mileage, fully comprehensive insurance, collision damage waiver and loss damage waiver. The company has drop-off points in most major cities, but will charge extra if you use a different one from that where you picked up the vehicle. A refuelling service charge will be applied if you do not replace the fuel you have used.

Underline or highlight the key words and expressions that helped you to identify the subject of each paragraph.

For reference see *Dictionary of Law* 4th edition (A & C Black 0-7475-6636-4).

Look at paragraphs 1 – 6 in the boxes, and answer the questions that follow them. Some of the words and expressions appeared in **Contracts 1** on pages 13 and 14.

1.

> This contract is <u>binding</u>, and we expect all the <u>parts</u> involved (both clients *and* suppliers) to <u>abide by</u> the <u>terms and conditions</u> stated in sections 3a – 37g on pages 1 – 17.

1. One of the <u>underlined</u> words / expressions in the above sentence is wrong. Identify and correct it.
2. True or false: a contract which is *binding* is flexible and can be changed at any time.
3. Two of these words / expressions could replace *abide by*. Which ones?
   (A) choose   (B) agree with   (C) obey   (D) change   (E) honour

2.

> On <u>terminator</u> of this contract, the company will be <u>obliged</u> to return any unused materials to the supplier within 28 days, unless <u>provision</u> has been made for a temporary extension. If any of the rules of the contract are <u>broken</u>, all materials must be returned immediately.

1. One of the <u>underlined</u> words / expressions in the above sentence is wrong. Identify and correct it.
2. True or false: *provision* has a similar meaning to *arrangement*.
3. Rearrange these letters to make two words which have a similar meaning to *obliged*:
   degabtlio   edequrir

3.

> The contract was originally <u>verbal</u>, but we've finally managed to get the company to give us something on paper. They say that this contract is <u>un-negotiable</u>, but maybe we can persuade them to <u>amend</u> some of the details before we sign <u>on the dotted line</u>.

1. One of the <u>underlined</u> words / expressions in the above paragraph is wrong. Identify and correct it.
2. True or false: the speaker thinks that it might be possible for small changes to be made to the contract before she signs it.
3. Rearrange the letters in **bold** to make words which have the same or a similar meaning to *verbal* in this situation
   rola   kosnep

4.

> Swillpot Airline Catering Ltd were <u>sued</u> by Pan-Globe Airways when they were found to be <u>in beach of their contract</u>, specifically that they had failed to <u>comply with</u> <u>clause</u> 27B, which stated that their food should be "fit for human consumption".

1. One of the <u>underlined</u> words / expressions in the above sentence is wrong. Identify and correct it.
2. Find a word or expression in paragraphs 1 – 3 above which has a similar meaning to *comply with* in paragraph 4.
3. True or false: Pan-Globe Airways are unhappy with Swillpot Airline Catering because they have breached *all* of their contractual terms.

For reference see *Dictionary of Law* 4th edition (A & C Black 0-7475-6636-4).

4.   Both Swillpot Airline Catering Ltd and Pan-Globe Airways signed the contract. In legal terms, would we describe the arrangement between the two companies as an **offer**, an **acceptance** or a **consideration**?

5.

> Withers Interiors Ltd have entered into an <u>agreement</u> with Sophos Construction to act as sole providers of quality interior fittings <u>commencing</u> 15 August this year. This is to run for 18 months, with a 3 month <u>period of notification</u> in the event of <u>cancellation</u> by either side.

1.   One of the <u>underlined</u> words / expressions in the above sentence is wrong. Identify and correct it.
2.   Which word in the paragraph is the closest in meaning to the noun *contract*?
3.   Is this an example of part of an *open-ended* contract?
4.   True or false: if either Withers Interiors Ltd or Sophos Construction want to end the contract, they must tell the other company 3 months before they do it.

6.

> This contract recognises the <u>anointment</u> of Mr Alan Wiley as non-executive Director to the board of AKL Publishing following the company's <u>amalgamation</u> with Berryhill Books. While Mr Wiley may continue to buy shares in the company, he may not acquire a <u>controlling interest</u>, and he may have no professional dealings with any <u>third parties</u> during this period.

1.   One of the <u>underlined words</u> / expressions in the above sentence is wrong. Identify and correct it.
2.   True or false: AKL Publishing recently separated from Berryhill Books.
3.   True or false: Mr Wiley can buy as many shares as he likes in the company.
4.   In addition to sitting on the board of AKL Publishing, how many other companies can Mr Wiley work for?

For reference see *Dictionary of Law* 4th edition (A & C Black 0-7475-6636-4).

Corporate responsibility 1: The environment

Corporate responsibility can broadly be defined as the responsibility a company or other organisation and its directors have to the people they employ, to their customers, to the people who live in and around their areas of operation and to the local, national and international environment. While many aspects of corporate responsibility are not laws in themselves, they may be part of, or become involved in, a legal process.

Complete this text about corporate responsibility and the environment with words from the box.

abused affected alternative assets benefit climate codes communities compensation conflict consultation degradation ecological ecosystems effect exploit extracts fossil genetically human rights impact implementing indigenous indirectly minimise non-renewable non-sustainable pollution precautions protocols reduce regulations regulatory renewable resources solar sustainable sustaining transparent voluntarily

A company should ensure that its actions do not damage local and global _____. It needs to _____ its use of natural _____ such as oil, gas and other _____ fuels, and regulate its _____ on aspects such as _____ change, and air, sea and noise _____ . It needs to be aware of the dangers it might pose in terms of _____ _____, and must follow local, national and international _____, rules, _____ and _____ designed to _____ damage. Where possible, it should _____ the availability of _____ power sources such as _____ and tidal power. If the company is involved in the agricultural sector, it should support and encourage _____ agriculture and forest use. If a company wishes to develop _____ modified products, it should do so only if it is safe, and only after public _____, and it should take all necessary _____. It should also have the approval of local people who might be _____. If accidents occur or _____ breaches are made, the company must be honest and _____ in its dealings with those who are affected, and assist them in _____ procedures to reduce its _____.

A company that _____ and exploits natural _____ resources such as coal, oil or gas, or _____ resources such as hydro-electric power, should ensure that it avoids _____ with local people, and that the _____ of those people are not _____ through its actions, either directly or _____. It needs to be aware of its role in _____ the environment, and helping to preserve the survival of local and national _____ (including _____ people who might be less able to represent or defend themselves). A company should avoid working in or around vulnerable and _____ communities unless its actions directly _____ those communities Where people are asked to move in order for a company to exploit local resources, they should do so _____, and should be offered adequate _____ for their land and _____ (the resource being exploited should be considered as one of these).

For reference see *Dictionary of Law* 4th edition (A & C Black 0-7475-6636-4).

Corporate responsibility 2: Communities

In this text, complete the *first* part of each word in **bold** with the second part of each word from the box.

___act ___ainability ___ation ___cipation ___ciples ___der ___diction
___ding ___ent ___erse ___ervation ___ests ___grate ___grity
___ial ___ibute ___icity ___ified ___ilities ___ision
___itted ___lated ___lations ___lement ___mental ___minate ___mote
___olve ___omic ___orce ___parency ___pect (x2) ___opment
___ply ___porate ___rdable ___tect ___ted ___ties ___traint ___ulate

A company should **res___**, **pro___** and **pro___** national and international human rights **trea___**, **prin___** and standards, regardless of whether or not these have been **rat___** by the host state, and regardless of whether or not such standards are legally-**bin___** in the host state. All companies should **reg___** their behaviour accordingly. A company should respect the political **juris___** of the host state, but where there are gross human rights **vio___** by the government of the host state, the company should withdraw its operations from that state.

A company should **com___** with internationally-recognised labour, health, safety and **environ___** standards. It should be **comm___** to ensuring that the communities it deals with and the people it employs are **trea___** with **res___**. It should recognise that its operations will have a **soc___**, **econ___** and environmental **imp___** on local communities, and it should **inv___** the community in any major **dec___**-making process. It should **contr___** to the **devel___** of that community, the **pres___** of local cultures, the development of social, educational and medical **fac___** and the **sust___** of the local economy. It should at all times **incor___** the best **inter___** of the community into its methods of operation, and actively encourage the **parti___** of the community in its operations.

If a company produces essential food or medical items to sell locally, it should **imp___** a policy of price **res___** so that these products are **affo___**. It should not charge grossly **inf___** prices. If the essential products it makes carry a **pat___**, the company should not **enf___** this if doing so will have an **adv___** effect on the health and wellbeing of local people.

A company should not **discri___** against, or **deni___**, local communities or individuals on the basis of race, **gen___**, culture, **ethn___**, religion, class, sexual **orient___** or disability.

A company should display **inte___** and **trans___** in *all* its operations at *all* times.

18

For reference see *Dictionary of Law* 4th edition (A & C Black 0-7475-6636-4).

Corporate responsibility 3: Employment

Look at this list of responsibilities a company should have for its employees. Then look at the notes about the company RJW Ltd on the next page. For each note, decide which responsibility is being ignored or abused. In some cases, there is more than one possible answer.

A.   A company should not discriminate on the grounds of gender, race, class, religion, disability, etc, when it comes to recruiting staff.

B.   A company should ensure that its employees are proportionally representative of the community in which it is based.

C.   A company should ensure that working hours are reasonable and that employees receive regular breaks.

D.   A company should ensure that its employees receive regular paid annual leave (and also maternity and compassionate leave when required).

E.   A company should provide equal pay for work of equal value.

F.   A company should pay a sustainable living wage to all of its employees.

G.   A company should provide adequate child-care facilities.

H.   A company should ensure that there is no physical, sexual or verbal harassment or abuse of workers.

I.   A company should ensure that health and safety rules are applied and closely followed.

J.   A company should not force its employees to have regular health checks, and then use the results to dismiss the employee.

K.   A company should not dismiss an employee on the grounds of pregnancy.

L.   A company should allow its employees to organise or join workers' organisations that represent their interests.

M.   A company should have a grievance procedure that is easy to understand and open to all employees.

N.   A company should provide adequate compensation for accidents and injuries sustained on its premises.

O.   A company should not dismiss or otherwise penalise an employee who refuses to work overtime.

P.   A company should not dismiss or otherwise penalise employees for failing to reach production targets.

Q.   A company should not use indentured, forced or slave labour, or employ anyone under duress.

R.   A company should ensure that an employee is dismissed as a last resort only, and only after verbal and written warnings.

For reference see *Dictionary of Law* 4th edition (A & C Black 0-7475-6636-4).

1. Several factory floor workers have been fired or had their wages reduced for refusing to stay and work late when needed.

2. Production manager Laurence Bailey broke his wrist when some unsecured panels fell on it. He is trying to get money out of the company for his injuries. 'You're not getting a penny out of this company,' his boss tells him. 'It's your problem, not ours'

3. Andrew Kelly is thinking of starting a union for the workers at RJW Ltd. The Company Director warns him that if he does, he will regretfully have to 'let him go'.

4. Manager Maureen Blake is always patting her male PA's backside and telling him he has 'a wonderful body'. He has complained several times, but nothing ever gets done about it.

5. Susie Roberts, a secretary for RJW Ltd, recently had a baby. She cannot afford a babysitter while she is at work, so the baby stays with her in the office.

6. RJW Ltd have their main office on the edge of an economically-deprived area predominantly inhabited by people of West Indian origin. The company prefers to hire white, male, middle class employees.

7. RJW Ltd has regular, compulsory medical check-ups for its employees. The company nurse believes that one of the workers, Charlie Higson, drinks a lot when off duty. She reports this to Charlie's manager, who then dismisses him.

8. Ron Smith and Emma Addams are sales executives for RJW Ltd. They both have the same qualifications and the same experience. Mr Smith receives £40,000 a year and Mrs Addams receives £34,000 a year.

9. Office assistant Tony White thinks his boss treats him badly. He wants to complain, but has no idea how to go about doing so. Nobody else seems to know what he should do either.

10. Factory-floor workers at RJW Ltd find it difficult to make ends meet. The cost of living is rising all the time, and the money they receive has not kept up with the rate of inflation.

11. Canteen assistant Anne Watkins oversleeps one morning and is two hours late for work. She has worked for RJW Ltd for 6 months and has never been late before. The canteen manager sacks her the moment she arrives.

12. Ellie McKenzie, a machine operator for RJW Ltd, works 12 hours a day with only 20 minutes for lunch.

13. Six months ago the company advanced one of its employees some money. When the employee became ill and was unable to pay back the money, the company insisted on using his children to work to pay off his debt.

14. Delivery driver Michael Blair is exhausted: he hasn't had a holiday for two years. The company says it cannot afford to give him the time off work.

15. Production assistant Richard Mann slipped on some oil on the factory floor, fell headlong through a glass panel, caught his arm in some unguarded machinery and was electrocuted by some exposed electrical wires.

16. Factory-floor workers have been told that a new quota system has been put in place: anyone who does not satisfy this quota will have their salaries reduced.

17. Accountant Audrey Jensen is delighted because she's just discovered she's going to have a baby. Her boss is not so happy: 'Sorry Audrey, you're fired,' he says.

For reference see *Dictionary of Law* 4th edition (A & C Black 0-7475-6636-4).

Financial and ethical integrity

Look at paragraphs 1 – 9 in the boxes, and do the task that accompanies each one.

Paragraph 1:

Find words in the paragraph below that mean:

1. To make something weaker or less effective
2. People who have invested in and own part of a business, or people who have a personal interest in how something happens
3. Open and honest about its actions
4. People who own shares in a company
5. Business dealings and other actions
6. To ask someone for something (in this case, for an immoral or unethical purpose)
7. Something which encourages
8. Money offered corruptly to someone to get him to do something to help you
9. Honesty / moral principles

> A company should not offer, solicit or accept bribes or any other form of financial incentive that could undermine its integrity, and for the sake of its shareholders and other stakeholders it should be transparent in all its accounting and financial transactions.

Paragraph 2:

This paragraph contains 7 wrong word *forms* (for example, a verb has been used instead of a noun, a singular form has been used when a plural form is necessary, etc). Identify and correct these words.

> A company should be social responsible in its investing, and exercise diligent to ensure that such investments do not have an adversity affect on human needs and right. It should be prepared to disclosure any information regarding its investments when asked to do so.

Paragraph 3:

Rearrange the letters in **bold** to make words.

> If a company **pssstecu** that it is being used for **minrilac** or other illegal activities, either from within the company or from the outside, it should report its **nssiosupci** to the relevant **rathouseiti** and put in place **rrserabi** to ensure that it does not happen again.

Paragraph 4:

Complete the paragraph with words or expressions from the first box.

> | disadvantaged | ensure | equitable | interest rates | policies |
> | predatory | profit margins | repayment | | |

> A company that lends money should avoid _____ practices such as imposing very high _____ and short _____ periods, especially in situations where people are particularly financially _____, and it should _____ that its lending _____ are _____, even if this means that they have to reduce their _____.

For reference see *Dictionary of Law* 4th edition (A & C Black 0-7475-6636-4).

Paragraph 5:

This paragraph contains 10 spelling mistakes. Identify and correct each one.

> A company should not infrange, copy or otherwise use without permision or acknoledgement a copywrite, a patient, a tradmark (registreed or otherwise) or anything else that could be construed as createive or intelectual propperty for financial gain.

Paragraph 6:

Read this paragraph, then do the task that follows it.

> A company should respect the rights of the individual to privacy and freedom from harassment, intimidation and any other act which could be viewed by the individual as an invasion of their privacy. In addition to maintaining good public relations with its customers, suppliers, and other people it works with, a company should also main good relations with its neighbours and people who live in and around its area of operations.

What is:
- The adjective form of the noun *privacy*?
- The verb form of the noun *harassment*?
- The adjective form of the noun *intimidation*?
- The verb form of the noun *invasion*?
- The noun form of the verb *maintaining*?
- The verb form of the noun / adjective *public*?
- The adjective form of the noun *neighbours*?

Paragraph 7:

Using your own words and ideas, explain the words and expressions in **bold** in this paragraph.

> As part of its **corporate governance** policy, a company should have clearly defined **codes of conduct**, **codes of best practice** and other **guidelines** for its directors and employees to follow and **uphold**.

Paragraphs 8 and 9:

Which words or expressions in paragraphs 8 and 9 below are closest in meaning to:
1. *disobeying*   2. *to end or finish*   3. *worries* (noun)   4. *to make something correct*
5. *to obey*   6. *to punish*   7. *negative effects or results*   8. *duties*

> A company should not penalise any employee for questioning its policies and its financial or ethical integrity, and employees should be aware that if they do so, there will be no repercussions. An employee should not have to comply with any rules that it feels undermine his / her, and the company's, integrity.
>
> The responsibilities in paragraphs 1 - 8 above should apply not only to the main company, but also to any of its subsidiaries, joint venture partners, suppliers, licensees, franchisees or investors. If a company believes that any of these are acting in an unethical way, or otherwise violating recognised ethical standards, it should address its concerns to the party involved and attempt to redress the situation. If necessary, the company should terminate its business relationships with the party or parties concerned.

For reference see *Dictionary of Law* 4th edition (A & C Black 0-7475-6636-4).

Court orders and injunctions

Choose the best word in bold to complete each of these sentences. Many of the expressions are particular to the law of England and Wales, but will probably have equivalents in other countries.

1. People who cause trouble in a particular place may be legally prevented from going to that place again. This is known as a **banning / bankruptcy** order.

2. In Britain, if someone is causing someone distress, harm or harassment, the police can apply for an **ASDA / ASBO** in order to restrict their behaviour.

3. In a civil case, a court may impose a **search / hunt** order allowing a party to inspect and photocopy or remove a defendant's documents, especially if the defendant might destroy those documents.

4. A promise given to a court (for example, by a vandal who promises not to damage property again) is known as an **undertaker / undertaking**.

5. Sometimes a temporary injunction can be imposed on someone until the case goes to court. This is known as a temporary or **interlocutory / interim** injunction.

6. A **restraining / restriction** order is a court order which tells a defendant not to do something while the court is still making a decision.

7. If someone applies for an injunction against a person with a mental disability, a third party will be appointed to act for that person. This third party is known as a litigation **assistant / friend**.

8. A **frozen / freezing** order or injunction prevents a defendant who has gone abroad from taking all his assets (for example, the money in his bank account) abroad (although he *is* allowed to take out money for living expenses).

9. If you want to stop a magazine publishing an article about you (or photographs of you) that you do not like, you can apply for a **publicity / publication** injunction.

10. A person who repeatedly harasses, pesters or hits another person might be given a **non-proliferation / non-molestation** order to prevent him / her from continuing to do it.

11. If your partner is trying to get you out of your shared home, or if he / she won't let you back into your home, you can apply for an **occupation / occupying** order to remain / get back into the home.

12. **Housing / Home** injunctions might protect you if you live in a council home and your neighbours are annoying and harassing you, or if you are a private tenant being harassed by your landlord.

13. A **Common / Public** Law injunction can sometimes be applied for if one partner of an unmarried couple is harassing, assaulting or trespassing on the property of the other.

14. **Reconstitution / Restitution** orders are court orders asking for property to be returned to someone.

15. An order of **discharge / disclosure** is a court order releasing someone from bankruptcy.

16. Many injunctions have a **penal / penalty** notice attached, which states that if the injunction is broken, the offender could be sent to prison.

17. Injunctions aimed at preventing violence may carry a power of **arrest / arrears** clause, which allows the police to take the offender into custody if the injunction is broken.

18. If an injunction is broken, **committal / committee** proceedings might follow: this is a process in which a court is asked to send the person who has broken the injunction to prison.

For reference see *Dictionary of Law* 4th edition (A & C Black 0-7475-6636-4).

Court structures

1. The United Kingdom

This plan shows a top-down representation of how the court system is structured in the United Kingdom. Test your knowledge of the system by rearranging the letters in **bold** to make words.

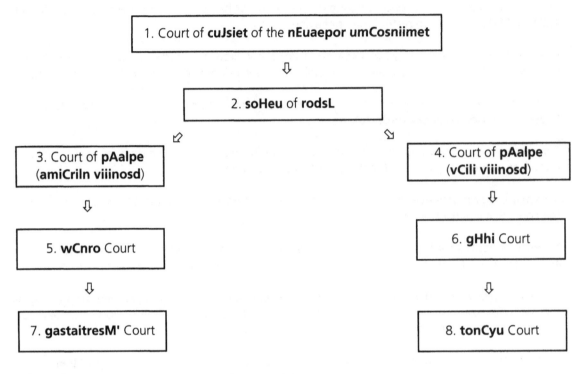

1. Court of **cuJsiet** of the **nEuaepor umCosniimet**

2. **soHeu** of **rodsL**

3. Court of **pAalpe** (**amiCriln viiinosd**)

4. Court of **pAalpe** (**vCili viiinosd**)

5. **wCnro** Court

6. **gHhi** Court

7. **gastaitresM'** Court

8. **tonCyu** Court

2. The USA

This plan shows a top-down representation of how the courts are structured in the USA. Test your knowledge of the system by rearranging the letters in **bold** to make words.

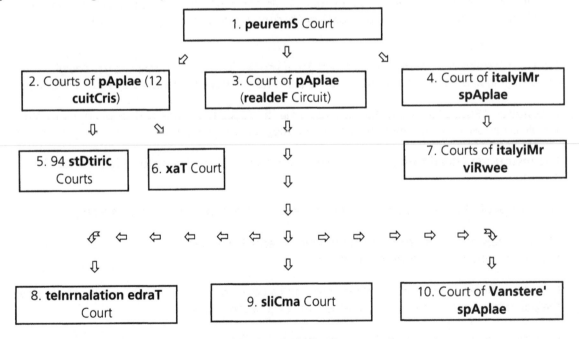

1. **peuremS** Court

2. Courts of **pAplae** (12 **cuitCris**)

3. Court of **pAplae** (**realdeF** Circuit)

4. Court of **italyiMr spAplae**

5. 94 **stDtiric** Courts

6. **xaT** Court

7. Courts of **italyiMr viRwee**

8. **teInrnalation edraT** Court

9. **sliCma** Court

10. Court of **Vanstere' spAplae**

24

For reference see *Dictionary of Law* 4th edition (A & C Black 0-7475-6636-4).

Crime 1: Crime categories

A crime is an illegal act which may result in prosecution and punishment by the state if the accused (= the person or people charged with a crime) is / are convicted (= found guilty in a court of law). Generally, in order to be convicted of a crime, the accused must be shown to have committed an illegal (= unlawful) act with a criminal state of mind.

Look at the list of crimes in the box, then look at the categories below. Decide which category each one comes under, and write the crime in the appropriate space in the table. Some crimes can be listed under more than one category. One of the words / expressions in the list is not a crime.

---

1. abduction   2. actual bodily harm   3. aiding and abetting (= assisting) an offender   4. arson
5. assault   6. battery   7. being equipped to steal   8. bigamy   9. blackmail
10. breach of the Official Secrets Act   11. breaking and entering   12. bribery   13. burglary
13. careless or reckless driving   14. committing a breach of the peace   15. conspiracy
16. contempt of court   17. criminal damage (vandalism, and sometimes also hooliganism)
18. deception or fraud in order to obtain property, services or pecuniary advantage
19. driving without a licence or insurance   20. drug dealing   21. drunk in charge / drink driving
22. embezzlement   23. espionage   24. forgery   25. grievous bodily harm
26. handling stolen goods   27. indecency   28. indecent assault   29. infanticide
30. manslaughter   31. misuse of drugs   32. money laundering   33. murder   34. obscenity
35. obstruction of the police   36. paedophilia   37. perjury   38. perverting the course of justice
39. piracy   40. possessing something with intent to damage or destroy property
41. possessing weapons   42. racial abuse   43. rape   44. robbery   45. sedition
46. suicide   47. terrorism   48. theft   49. treason   50. unlawful assembly   51. wounding

---

Crimes against the person

Crimes against property

Public order offences

Road traffic offences

Sexual offences

Political offences

Offences against justice

For reference see *Dictionary of Law* 4th edition (A & C Black 0-7475-6636-4).

Crime 2: Name the offence

Look at these situations, then decide which crime has been, or is being, committed in each case. These crimes can all be found in Crime 1 on page 29, but try to do this exercise first without referring back. In some cases, more than one option is possible. (Note that you do not need to use all of the crimes from page 29).

1. *TV Newsreader*: Police believe the fire was started deliberately at around 2 o'clock this morning when burning paper was pushed through the letterbox. They are appealing for witnesses to the event.

2. Crown *Prosecutor*: Tell us in your own words exactly what happened.
   Witness: We were in the bar when a man walked up to the victim, pointed a gun at his head and said 'You're a dead man.' Then he pulled the trigger three times.

3. *Police constable*: You were going in excess of 60, and this is a 30 zone.
   Man in car: I think you're mistaken, constable. I was well within the speed limit.

4. *Woman*: When I got home, I discovered that my back door had been broken open.
   Police officer: Had anything been stolen?
   Woman: Yes, my new laptop, £200 in cash and my pet parrot.

5. *Police officer*: I'm sorry sir, but I have to report your actions to the proper authorities.
   Man: Look, officer, here's £50. Let's just pretend this didn't happen, eh?

6. *Extract from a newspaper article*: The two men were arrested and detained after police checks revealed that they had been distributing pornographic material over the Internet.

7. *Interviewing detective*: All right, Dagsy. We know you didn't do the Cornmarket Street bank job yourself, but we know that you were involved somehow.
   Police suspect: I was just driving the car Mr Regan, honest. And I didn't know what the others were up to until they came back with bags of cash.

8. *TV newsreader*: The car bomb went off in a busy marketplace, injuring several shoppers.

9. *Radio newsreader*: The police raided a house in New Street this morning and recovered 250 illegal copies of the latest Harry Potter film, along with professional film copying equipment.

10. *Man reading newspaper*: I don't believe it. The Foreign Minister has been caught giving government secrets to another country!

11. *Political agitator*: Now is the time to rise up and overthrow the running dogs that call themselves our government. Death to the Prime Minister and his cronies! Death to the Royal Family! Death to the system that bleeds us dry and abandons us!
    Unwashed anarchist hordes: Hooray!

12. *Shop assistant*: I can't accept this £20 note, madam. It's a fake.
    Customer: What? You mean it's counterfeit?
    Shop assistant: I'm afraid so. Do you have any other means of payment?

13. *Extract from a newspaper article*: The investigation into the rail accident confirmed that it occurred because the rail company had failed to maintain the tracks properly over a five-year period. Eight people died when the train left the tracks and hit an embankment.

For reference see *Dictionary of Law* 4th edition (A & C Black 0-7475-6636-4).

14. *Police officer*: Take your time and tell me what happened, dear.
    Pensioner: The man who came to my door said he had come to read the electric meter,
    so I let him in. I went to the kitchen to make him a cup of tea. When I returned he had gone, and
    so had my television.

15. *TV newsreader*: A journalist working in the city disappeared this morning. Police later received a
    note from a militant faction claiming that they had taken him and were holding him hostage.

16. *Woman*: The graffiti around here is getting really bad. Last week somebody wrote 'Chelsea are
    rubbish' on our garden wall.
    Man: That's not good. It should say 'Chelsea are complete rubbish'.

17. *Man*: Look at this note, Cheri. It arrived in the post today. It says 'Leave £10,000 in cash in the bin
    by the bus stop, or I'll tell everyone your dirty secret'.
    Woman: Don't worry about it, Tony. It's probably another little joke from him next door.

18. *Prosecuting lawyer*: Tell us again what happened on the night of the incident, Mr Williams. And let
    me remind you that you are still under oath.
    Defendant: Like I told you, I was at home asleep, so I have no idea what happened.
    Prosecuting lawyer: Don't lie, Mr Williams. We have video evidence that you were in the nightclub
    until 3am. And you were seen by several witnesses.

19. *Defendant*: I don't recognise this court. This trial shouldn't be taking place.
    Judge: Sit down, Mr Dowling. You are out of order.
    Defendant: Oh shut up, you silly old woman. Go back home and do some washing up or
    something.

20. *Accountant*: We've audited these accounts very carefully, and they just don't add up.
    Office manager: What exactly are you saying?
    Accountant: I'm saying that someone in your office has been secretly helping themselves to
    company money.

21. *TV presenter*: Jimmy Bond, a former government intelligence agent, has just published a book
    about the Intelligence Service called 'Lifting the Lid'. In it, he gives us a revealing insight into the
    life of a secret agent. The government have strongly condemned the book, claiming it contains
    classified information that should not be in the public domain.

22. *Magistrate*: Constable, could you explain what happened?
    Police constable: I was proceeding down Newland Street at approximately 8 o'clock last night
    when I heard a lot of shouting coming from The Newlands Inn public house. On entering, I saw the
    accused in a state of undress and dancing on a table.
    Magistrate: You mean he was naked?
    Police constable: Yes. As the day he was born.

23. *Radio newsreader*: The judge in the trial of notorious gangster Joe 'Pinko' Pallino adjourned the
    court today after it was revealed that several members of the jury had been offered bribes and
    other incentives to pass a verdict of 'not guilty' on Mr Pallino.

24. *TV presenter*: A bank account was opened in a false name in the Bahamas, and the cash deposited
    there. The funds were then sent by telegraphic transfer to another account in Switzerland, and the
    Bahamas account was closed. It was at this stage that the Metropolitan Police called in Interpol.

For reference see *Dictionary of Law* 4th edition (A & C Black 0-7475-6636-4).

Crime 3: Criminal procedure (part 1)

Imagine that a crime has taken place. Look at sentences 1 – 15 (which explain what happens next) and rearrange the letters in **bold** to make words and expressions. The first letter of each word / expression is in the correct place. Note that one word is used twice, but with a different meaning.

1. Once the crime has been **cedmitomt**, it is **rotpeder** to the police by the **vitmic**.

2. The police arrive at the **sneec** of the crime to **itsanetiveg** what has happened.

3. They look for important **cesul** and other **ecdnevie** (for example, fingerprints or a genetic profile) that will help them to identify the **crupitl**.

4. In some cases, they will also try to establish if the **mudso odiranpe** (a Latin expression which describes the way in which the crime was carried out) matches other crimes in the area.

5. If they have a **stupsce** who doesn't have a good **iblia**, they will then **arepnhedp** him*.

6. When he is **artsrede**, the police will **conutia** him (in other words, they warn him that anything he says might be used later in court).

7. He is then taken to the police station, where he is **iewervinted** by the **iigengstatinv oerfsicf**.

8. He is allowed to have a **sitocirol** present if he wants.

9. If he wants **lagle ratprstionneee** at this stage, but cannot afford it, the police must provide it.

10. If, at the end of the interview, the police believe that they have the right man, they **ceragh** him with the crime.

11. A **stemnttae** is prepared, which is signed by all parties present.

12. The **ascedcu** is then either **redseale** on bali (in other words, he is allowed to leave the police station and go home in exchange for a financial 'deposit', on condition that he promises to appear in court when required: if he doesn't appear in court, he will lose this deposit and a **twrraan** will be issued for his arrest), or he is **rdaeedmn** in **cysodut** and locked in a cell to prevent him from running away.

13. More questioning will probably follow: the police need as much **pofor** as possible (anything that is **assdblimie** in court will help them to get a **cinonctivo**), and they may also be interested in any **apcosmiccel** who may have helped their man.

14. The police will also want to talk to any **wisestsen** who were present when the crime took place.

15. The next day, the man appears before a **metgiasrat** in a **metgiasrats**' court. If the police present their **csea** properly and have followed all the correct procedures and protocols, he will then be **cedmitomt** for **tirla** at a **Conwr** Court.

* or *her*, of course!

For reference see *Dictionary of Law* 4th edition (A & C Black 0-7475-6636-4).

Crime 4: Criminal procedure (part 2)

Before you do this exercise, see **Crime 3** on the previous page.

Here are the various stages of a criminal trial. Read through them, and try to remember as much information as possible. Then cover this page, and try to complete the same sentences on the next page with the information that has been removed.

When the accused knows that he is going to stand trial, he asks a solicitor to prepare his case.

The information collected is then given to a barrister who will defend him in court.

In a criminal case, the police will have their own barrister, who is known as the *Crown Prosecutor*.

These two barristers are referred to throughout the trial as *counsel for the defence* and *counsel for the prosecution*.

Before the trial begins, the counsels review their evidence and decide how to present their case.

Members of the jury, when required, are selected and briefed on their duties. A date for the trial is arranged.

At the beginning of the trial, the judge asks the defendant how he pleads: 'guilty' or 'not guilty'.

Both counsels then address the jury with a summary of what they believe is true, and explain what the jury will hear at the trial.

The counsel for the prosecution then calls and questions witnesses. The counsel for the defence can cross-examine these people. The defendant will also be questioned by both counsels.

At the end of the trial, the counsels summarise the facts as they see them, and the jury then retires to deliberate in private.

When the jury has reached its verdict, it returns to the court and the foreman of the jury delivers the verdict to the court.

If the defendant is found to be 'not guilty', he is acquitted.

However, if the jury's verdict is 'guilty', the defendant is convicted and sentenced by the judge.

The defendant may have to serve a custodial sentence (in other words go to prison), he may be given a suspended sentence, or he may be fined (or a combination of two of these).

If the defendant is not happy with the decision of the court, he is free to appeal to a higher court. The highest courts for appellants in England and Wales are the House of Lords and the Court of Justice of the European Communities (also called the European Court of Justice, or ECJ for short).

For reference see *Dictionary of Law* 4th edition (A & C Black 0-7475-6636-4).

When you are doing this exercise, try not to refer back to the previous page until you have completed it.

When the _____ knows that he is going to stand trial, he asks a _____ to prepare his _____.

The information collected is then given to a _____ who will _____ him in court.

In a criminal case, the police will have their own barrister, who is known as the _____ (2 words).

These two barristers are referred to throughout the trial as _____ (4 words) and _____ (4 words).

Before the trial begins, the counsels review their _____ and decide how to present their case.

Members of the _____, when required, are selected and _____ on their duties. A date for the trial is arranged.

At the beginning of the trial, the judge asks the defendant how he _____: '_____' or '_____' (2 words).

Both counsels then address the jury with a _____ of what they believe is true, and explain what the jury will hear at the trial.

The counsel for the prosecution then calls and _____ _____. The counsel for the defence can _____(2 words joined by a hyphen) these people. The defendant will also be questioned by both counsels.

At the end of the trial, the counsels summarise the facts as they see them, and the jury then _____ to _____ in private.

When the jury has reached its _____, it returns to the court and the _____ of the jury delivers it to the court.

If the defendant is found to be 'not guilty', he is _____.

However, if the jury's verdict is 'guilty', the defendant is _____ and _____ by the judge.

The defendant may have to serve a _____ sentence (in other words go to prison), he may be given a _____ sentence, or he may be _____ (or a combination of two of these).

If the defendant is not happy with the decision of the court, he is free to _____ to a higher court. The highest courts for _____ in England and Wales are the House of _____ and the Court of Justice of the European Communities (also called the European Court of Justice, or _____ for short).

For reference see *Dictionary of Law* 4th edition (A & C Black 0-7475-6636-4).

Dispute resolution

Commercial and business *disputes* (= arguments / disagreements between two or more parties) do not necessarily have to be settled in an imposed court case. *Mediation* – an attempt by a third party to make two sides in an argument agree – is often quicker, cheaper, more effective and less stressful for the parties involved.

Complete the first part of each word in **bold** in sentences 1 – 18 with the second part in the box.

___actually	___ain	___artial	___bunal	___cation	___closed	___cus	___dential
___ding	___ficial	___gation	___iator	___int	___itator	___judice	___lements
___lic	___native	___our	___promise	___sent	___sion	___tiations	___tical
___tration	___trator	___ual	___und	___untary	___utions		

1. Mediation is one form of what is known as **alter____** dispute resolution (ADR for short).

2. Mediation is generally preferable to **liti____** because it is normally quicker and cheaper.

3. Mediation is **vol____**, but requires the **con____** of all the parties involved before it can go ahead.

4. Mediation is carried out by a neutral, **imp____** third party called a **med____**.

5. This third party is also sometimes known as a **facil____**.

6. He / she spends time with all the parties involved in **jo___ ses____** and also in private meetings (known as '**cau___**').

7. Any information that the parties provide is **confi___** and cannot be **dis____** to the other parties.

8. He / she attempts to solve problems and find **resol____** that are **prac____** and **bene____** to everyone.

9. Unlike a formal court case, **nego____** are in private.

10. Resolutions and **sett____** are based on **com____** and on **mut____** agreement and acceptance.

11. If no agreement is reached, the parties involved will not be legally **bo____** by anything that has been discussed.

12. A mediation process is said to be 'without **pre____**', which means that anything that was said during the mediation cannot be used if there is no agreement and the case has to go to court.

13. If an agreement is reached and the parties sign a written agreement, this agreement becomes **bin____**, and the parties are obliged to **hon____** it. This can then be enforced **contr____** if necessary.

14. Another form of ADR is **arbi____**.

15. This will involve all parties in the dispute appearing before a **tri____**.

16. An **arbi____** is usually an expert in a particular field, and so this form of dispute resolution may be preferable in disputes where specialist knowledge is required.

17. However, unlike mediation, this form of resolution involves an **adjudi____**, which will probably benefit one side in the dispute more than the other(s).

18. This form of dispute resolution is also less private than mediation (each party is aware of what the other party is saying about it), and information may end up in the **pub____ dom___**.

For reference see *Dictionary of Law* 4th edition (A & C Black 0-7475-6636-4).

Employment and human resources

Read these extracts, then find words or expressions in them to match the definitions on the next page. The words / expressions are in the same order as the definitions.

A company manager is talking to a newspaper about his company structure:
The company has over 200 employees on its payroll. Some are employed part-time mornings only, Monday to Friday, and some are employed full-time (Monday to Friday 9 to 5). Everyone is given a contract before they start work outlining their duties and responsibilities, and what they can expect from the company in return. Every employee receives at least the minimum wage. We pride ourselves on being an equal-opportunities employer.

From an Internet page on employees' rights:
If an employer no longer needs an employee (because, for example, the company is closing down or moving) and has to dismiss him, then the employee is entitled to receive redundancy pay. Many companies will try to provide employees with suitable alternative employment.

From a factory-floor notice on employers' liability and employees' responsibilities:
Health and safety regulations are very important and must be followed at all times. The company believes that all employees should have maximum protection against industrial accidents. The company will not be held liable for injuries and disabilities sustained as a result of poor working practices by employees, and will accept no liability for these in the event of any claims for compensation. The company has a scale of fixed monetary awards to compensate those employees who are affected by accidents caused as a result of company negligence. In the event of an employee's death, any awards due will be passed on to the employee's dependants.

From a website explaining working time regulations:
An employee cannot be compelled to work for more than 48 hours a week over a 17-week period. If an employer makes him work more than this time, the employee can complain to an employment tribunal. Employees must also be allowed to take 24 hours off work every 7 days, and take a minimum 20-minute break if their working day exceeds 6 hours. They must also be allowed a rest period of 11 consecutive hours in every 24 hours. All employees are entitled to paid annual leave, regardless of how long they have worked for a company.

From a leaflet explaining women's rights at work:
Women cannot be dismissed on the grounds of pregnancy or childbirth. They are entitled to up to 26 weeks maternity leave, and to receive maternity pay during this period. If a woman has completed 26 weeks of continuous service with her employer by the beginning of the 14th week before the expected birth of her child, she can take another 26 weeks: this is usually unpaid, but some companies will make contributions. She must give her employer at least 28 days' notice of the date on which she intends to begin her leave. Women are also allowed to take reasonable time off work before the child is born for antenatal care. If a company has to suspend a woman on the grounds of maternity (because, for example, the work she is doing might endanger the unborn child), it must offer her alternative employment or continue to pay her normal salary.
(Note that fathers are entitled to two weeks' paid paternity leave. Both parents can also take another 13 weeks' unpaid parental leave).

A union leader is addressing some new employees:
Discrimination and harassment of any kind (sexual, racial, etc) will not be tolerated in this company, and are sackable offences, as are bullying and intimidation. If any employee has a genuine grievance in regard to these, or other, problems, you should talk to me or talk directly to your line manager. We will take such allegations very seriously, and will talk you through the grievance procedure so that you know the options that are open to you.

For reference see *Dictionary of Law* 4th edition (A & C Black 0-7475-6636-4).

1. People who are employed by someone else.

2. The list of people employed and paid by a company.

3. Not working for the whole working week.

4. Working for the whole working week.

5. A legal agreement between two or more parties.

6. The work which a person has to do.

7. The lowest hourly amount of money that a company can pay its employees.

8. A situation where everyone is treated the same.

9. A person or company who employs someone.

10. To remove an employee from a job.

11. To give or have the right to do something.

12. A situation where someone is no longer employed because the company no longer needs him / her.

13. Something which takes the place of something else.

14. An area of employment policy that deals with the well-being of employees at work.

15. Rules.

16. Something or legislation which protects.

17. Accidents which happen at work.

18. Legally responsible for something.

19. Physical hurt caused to somebody.

20. The condition of being unable to use part of the body.

21. Payment made by someone to cover the cost of damage or hardship.

22. Relating to money.

23. The failure to give proper care to something, especially a duty or responsibility, with the result that a person or property is harmed.

24. Someone who is supported financially by someone else.

25. To be made or forced to do something against your will.

26. A special court outside the judicial system which examines special problems and makes judgements.

27. To be more than a particular number or amount.

28. Without interruption.

29. Holiday or other period of work.

30. The state of expecting to give birth.

31. The act of giving birth.

32. A period when a woman is away from work to have a baby.

33. Payment made by an employer to an employee who is away from work to have a baby.

34. Money paid to add to a sum that already exists, or money paid to help someone do something.

35. The time allowed before something can take place.

36. Before giving birth.

37. To stop someone working for a period of time.

38. A period when a man is away from work because his partner is having a baby.

39. Adjective referring to parents.

40. The unfair treatment of someone because of their race, colour, class, etc.

41. The action of worrying, bothering or frightening someone.

42. A complaint made by an employee to an employer.

43. A statement, usually given in evidence, that something is true.

44. The steps an employee goes through if he / she has a complaint.

For reference see *Dictionary of Law* 4th edition (A & C Black 0-7475-6636-4).

European courts, institutions, etc

Each of the sections on Europe below contain either spelling mistakes, wrong words, or wrong word forms. Identify and correct these words in each case.

The European Union (EU)

(*This section contains 6 mistakes*)

This is a group of European notions that form a single economical community and have agreed on socialist and political cooperation. There are currently 25 member states. The Union has a Parliment and a main execution body called the European Commission (which is made up of members nomminated by each member state).

The Council of Europe

(*This section contains 5 mistakes*)

This is one of the four bodies which form the basis of the European Union. The Council does not have fixed members, but the member states are each represented by the relevant goverment minister. The Council is headed by a President, and the Presidencey rotates among the member states in alphabetical order, each serving a six-month period. This means that in effect each member can control the aggenda of the Council, and therefore that of the European Union during their six-month period, and can try to get as many of its proposings put into legislative as it can.

The European Convention on Human Rights

(*This section contains 8 mistakes*)

This is a convention signed by all members of the Council of Europe covering the rights and fundamentally freedoms of all its citizens, and aims to prevent violents and beaches of human rights. The convention recognises property rights, the right of citizens to privately, the due progress of law and the principal of legal review or appal. The key provisions are now incorporated by the Human Rights Act of 1998, which came into farce in the United Kingdom in October 2000.

The European Court of Human Rights

(*This section contains 9 mistakes*)

This is a court that considers the rights of citizens of states which are parts to the European Convention for the protecting of human rights, and has jurisprudence over cases that cannot be setled by the European Commission of Human Rights (see below). It protects many base rights, including the right to life, freedom from fear, freedom from torture, freedom of speaking, freedom of religion worship, freedom of assemblage and asociation, etc (in fact, most of the articles in the *Universal Declaration of Human Rights*, on which the European Convention is based: see the section on Human Rights on pages 44 – 48). Its formal name is the European Court for the Protection of Human Rights.

For reference see *Dictionary of Law* 4th edition (A & C Black 0-7475-6636-4).

The European Commission of Human Rights
(*This section contains 5 mistakes*)

This is a body which invettigates any breaches and abusings of the European Convention on Human Rights. It attempts to end griefances, especially if they contraveen the articles detailed in the European Convention, and to help agrievved parties reach a settlement without recourse to the European Court of Human Rights (see above).

The European Court of Justice (the ECJ)
(*This section contains 10 mistakes*)

This is a court set up to see that the principles of law as laid out in the Treaty of Rome are observed and applicated correctly in the European Union, and has juristic over issues of European Law. Its full name is the *Court of Justice of the European Communities*. The Court is responsible for settling dispites relating to European Union law, and also acting as a last Court of Appeal against judgementals in individual member states.

Court judges in the ECJ are apointed by the governments of the member states for a period of six years. These judges come from all the member states, and bring with them the legality traditions of each state. The court can either meet as a full court, or in chombers where only two or three judges are present. The court normally conducts its business in French, although if an acting is brought before the court by or against a member state, the member state can choose the language in which the case will be heard. The court can hear actions against institutionals, or actions brought either by the Commission or by a member state against another member state. The court also acts as Court of Appeal for appeals from the Court of First Instance (CFI). The court also interprets legislation and as such acts in a semi-legislationary capacity.

Note: most of the mistakes in this exercise are typical of mistakes made through carelessness. Always check your written work for similar mistakes. Remember that in law, careful and specific use of words (and their forms and spellings) is very important. A wrong word or a wrong spelling could change everything!

For reference see *Dictionary of Law* 4th edition (A & C Black 0-7475-6636-4).

The family 1: Relationships

Test your knowledge with this quiz.

1. A contract between a man and a woman to become husband and wife is called a / an:
    (a) wedding   (b) engagement   (c) marriage   (d) affair   (e) relationship

2. Rearrange the letters in **bold** to make a word meaning *husband* or *wife*: **pusoes**

3. True or false: If you have a *partner*, you are assumed to be *married*.

4. Are *same-sex marriages* legal in Britain?

5. What is the difference between a *separation* and a *divorce*?

6. Complete this sentence with the appropriate word in **bold**:
    The judge decided that the marriage had never been legal and so he **annexed / antedated / annulled** it (in other words, he declared that it had no legal effect).

7. What is the name we give to the notifiable offence of going through a ceremony of marriage to someone when you are still married to someone else? Is it:
    (a) monogamy   (b) bigamy   (c) polygamy   (d) monotony

8. In England and Wales, what kind of court deals with divorces? Is it:
    (a) a magistrates' court   (b) a Crown Court   (c) a High Court   (d) a County Court
    (e) a court of appeal

9. In England and Wales, a divorce can only be granted on one condition (known as *grounds for divorce*): that the *marriage has broken down irretrievably* (in other words, it cannot be made right again). Here are two of the conditions necessary for an irretrievable breakdown:

    (1) The couple have lived apart for two years and both consent to divorce.
    (2) The couple have lived apart for five years and no consent from the other spouse is needed.

    Rearrange the letters in bold to make words for the other conditions:

    (3) **tdyulera** by one spouse   (4) **runbesaleona brvioeuha** of a spouse
    (5) **soedernti** by one spouse

10. Here is a simplified version of the main divorce procedure. Complete the gaps with words from the box.

    ┌───┐
    │   affidavit   decree absolute   decree nisi   dispute (x3)   │
    │   petition (x2)   petitioner (x2)   respondent (x2)   │
    └───┘

    A request (a _____) is made by the _____ (= *the person applying for the divorce*) to the court for a divorce, in which the facts about the people involved and the reasons for the divorce are explained.

    The court sends the divorce _____ to the _____ (= *the other spouse*), together with a form called an *Acknowledgement of Service* form, which he / she completes. In it, he / she indicates whether or not he / she wishes to _____ the divorce.

    He / She returns this to the court within 7 days. (If he / she wants to _____ the divorce and / or its terms, he / she is sent another form to complete).

For reference see *Dictionary of Law* 4th edition (A & C Black 0-7475-6636-4).

Assuming that the _____ does not want to _____ the divorce or the terms, a copy of the Acknowledgement of Service form is sent to the _____, who confirms the facts sent in their original petition by swearing an _____.

The court pronounces the _____, an order ending the marriage subject to a full _____, which comes later and ends the marriage completely.

11. If a divorced couple have children, one of them may be required to make regular payments to their ex-husband / ex-wife to help pay for the upbringing of the children. What are these payments called? Are they:
(a) child support   (b) child maintenance   (c) child benefit   (d) child pensions

12. Look at this situation:
An <u>unmarried</u> couple with two children separate. The father moves away to another town. Is he legally obliged to make payments to his ex-partner for the upbringing of the children?

13. In England and Wales, the agency responsible for the assessment, review, collection and enforcement of payments is called the *CSA*. What do you think these letters stand for?

14. If a parent refuses to pay money for the upbringing of his / her ex-partner's children, the CSA can ask a court to make an *Attachment of Earnings Order*. What do you think this is?

15. How old should children be before a CSA ruling no longer applies? Is it:
(a) 15   (b) 16   (c) 17   (d) 18

16. What is *alimony*? Is it:
(a) money that a court orders a husband to pay regularly to his separated or divorced wife
(b) money that a court orders a father to pay regularly to his children until they are old enough to leave home
(c) money that the state pays a married couple to help them pay for a divorce
(d) money that a married couple must save to pay for their children's education

17. If a couple are <u>unmarried</u>, and one of them dies, who gets their estate (land, money and possessions) if the deceased (the dead person) has not made a will? Is it:
(a) the deceased's partner
(b) the deceased's immediate family
(c) the state

18. Who is your *next of kin*?

For reference see *Dictionary of Law* 4th edition (A & C Black 0-7475-6636-4).

The family 2: Children

Exercise 1:

Complete this definition and explanation (which has been adapted from the A & C Black *Dictionary of Law*) with words and expressions from the box.

adult	binding	business	convicted	guardians	Juvenile	juveniles	land
legal status	majority	malice	marry	minor	minority	parents	responsible
vote	will	written permission	young offender	young person	Youth

A child can be defined as 'a person under the age of 18'. We can also use the word '_____'. The state of being less than 18 years old is called '_____'. When a child becomes 18, he / she reaches the age of _____ and so is legally regarded as an _____. In other words, he/ she becomes _____ for his / her own actions, can sue, be sued or undertake _____ transactions.

In Great Britain a child does not have full _____ until the age of 18. A contract is not _____ on a child, and a child cannot own _____, cannot make a _____, cannot _____ and cannot drive a car (under the age of seventeen). A child cannot _____ before the age of 16, and can only do so between the ages of 16 and 18 with the _____ of his / her _____ or legal _____. A child who is less than 10 years old is not considered capable of committing a crime; a child between 10 and 14 years of age may be considered capable of doing so if there is evidence of _____ or knowledge, and so children of these ages can in certain circumstances be _____. In criminal law the term 'child' is used for children between the ages of 10 and 14; for children between 14 and 17, the term '_____' is used; all children are termed '_____'. If someone between these ages commits a crime, he / she is known as a _____, and may be sentenced in a _____ Court (previously known as a _____ Court).

Exercise 2:

1.   Choose the correct word in **bold** to complete this sentence:
      The money paid by the state to a person who is responsible for a child under 16 years of age is called child **support / maintenance / benefit / pension**.

2.   When two people divorce or get separated and one of them has care of their children, the other has the right to see the child regularly. True or false: this is called **excess**.

3.   True or false: in Britain, the responsibility for the assessment, review, collection and enforcement of maintenance for children is supervised by the courts.

4.   What does the Latin expression '*in loco parentis*' mean?

5.   Rearrange the letters in bold to make a word: A child or young person who acts in an antisocial way or breaks the law is known as a **queendltin**.

6.   Choose the best meaning of the word *adoption*. Is it:
      (a) the act of looking after and bringing up a child who is not your own
      (b) the act of becoming the legal parent of a child which is not your own
      (c) the act of having your children supervised while they are at home to make sure they are being well cared for

For reference see *Dictionary of Law* 4th edition (A & C Black 0-7475-6636-4).

7.   Which of the following are allowed to be foster parents?:
       (a) married couples   (b) unmarried couples   (c) single women   (d) single men
       (e) same-sex couples

8.   Complete the words in **bold**: If a parent or guardian fails to provide a child with adequate shelter,
       food, clothing, medical attention and supervision, this is known as **n** _ _ _ _ _ _. If a parent
       intentionally harms a child physically or mentally, this is known as **a** _ _ _ _.

9.   Choose the correct word in **bold** to complete this sentence:
       Sometimes, if a woman is physically unable to conceive and have a baby, the couple may ask
       another woman to have the baby for them and then give the baby to them: this woman is known
       as a **surrogate / surreal / surety / surrender** mother.

10.   What is a **Guardian ad Litem**? Is it:
       (a) a parent who does not live with his / her child.
       (b) a child who does not have a parent or legal guardian.
       (c) a person appointed by a court to represent a child in a legal action.

11.   True or false: a parent can be held legally responsible for the actions of their children if the
       children do something wrong or illegal.

12.   True or false: if *one* parent in a couple is found guilty of the offences in number 8 above, a court
       can apply to have the parent taken out of the family home rather than the child.

13.   *Truancy* is becoming a major problem in Britain. What do you think this word means?

14.   In Britain there are various orders that can be applied for children in different situations. Match the
       order 1 – 8 with what it does (a) – (h):

       1. Care Order   2. Supervision Order   3. Search and Find Order   4. Disclosure Order
       5. Prohibited Steps Order   6. Specific Issue Order   7. Contact Order   8. Residence Order

       (a) If the parents cannot decide what to do about major issues related to their children, they can let
       a court decide for them.
       (b) In cases of separation and divorce, this decides who the child will live with (in other words, who
       gets custody of the child)
       (c) The court can prevent one parent from taking a child away from the other parent (often used if
       there is a danger the parent will take the child out of the country).
       (d) A court can order the police or other legally-appointed body to enter a house where they think
       a child might be held against his / her will, in bad conditions, or illegally by a person not entitled to
       look after the child.
       (e) A separated or divorced parent wants to see his / her children (who are living with the other
       parent) for short periods on a regular basis.
       (f) The local social services regularly visit the home to check that children are being well cared for.
       (g) If a person knows where a child is being illegally held, they must give this information to the
       police or the court, or face prosecution.
       (h) Children are taken away from their home and parents / guardians by the local social services.

For reference see *Dictionary of Law* 4th edition (A & C Black 0-7475-6636-4).

Human rights 1

The *Universal Declaration of Human Rights* was proclaimed and adopted by the General Assembly of the United Nations in 1948. It details the rights of individual men and women to basic freedoms such as freedom of speech, freedom of religious worship, freedom from fear and hunger, etc. The Declaration has 30 sections, or *articles*.

Exercise 1:
Here are the first ten articles in their original form. Read through them, then match words in the articles with the dictionary definitions 1 – 27 below the box. The words are in the same order as the definitions.

Article 1: All human beings are born free and equal in dignity and rights. They are endowed with reason and conscience and should act towards one another in a spirit of brotherhood.

Article 2: Everyone is entitled to all the rights and freedoms set forth in this declaration, without distinction of any kind, such as race, colour, sex, language, religion, political or other opinion, national or social origin, property, birth or other status. Furthermore, no distinction shall be made on the basis of the political, jurisdictional or international status of the country or territory to which a person belongs, whether it be independent, trust, non-self-governing or under any other limitation of sovereignty.

Article 3: Everyone has the right to life, liberty and security of freedom.

Article 4: No one shall be held in slavery or servitude; slavery and the slave trade shall be prohibited in all their forms.

Article 5: No one shall be subjected to torture or to cruel, inhuman or degrading treatment or punishment.

Article 6: Everyone has the right to recognition everywhere as a person before the law.

Article 7: All are equal before the law and are entitled without any discrimination to equal protection of the law. All are entitled to equal protection against any discrimination in violation of this declaration and against any incitement to such discrimination.

Article 8: Everyone has the right to an effective remedy by the competent national tribunals for acts violating the fundamental rights granted him / her by the constitution or by law.

Article 9: No one shall be subjected to arbitrary arrest, detention or exile.

Article 10: Everyone is entitled in full equality to a fair and public hearing by an independent and impartial tribunal, in the determination of his / her rights and obligations and of any criminal charge against him / her.

1. The same (adjective)
2. The things that you should be allowed to have (noun)
3. A feeling you have that you have done right or wrong (noun)
4. To have the right to do or have something (verb)
5. Difference (noun)
6. A group of people with distinct physical characteristics or culture (noun)
7. Referring to government or party politics (adjective)
8. Having the legal power over someone or something (adjective)

For reference see *Dictionary of Law* 4th edition (A & C Black 0-7475-6636-4).

9. The act of limiting something (noun)
10. The situation of being free (noun)
11. The situation of being a person who belongs to someone and works for them without payment (noun)
12. The situation of having to work very hard for someone, usually in poor conditions and with very little or no pay (noun)
13. The buying and selling of people against their will (noun: 2 words)
14. To say that something must not happen (verb)
15. Hurting someone badly so that they are forced to give information (noun)
16. Causing fear, anguish and inferiority (adjective)
17. The unfair treatment of someone because of their colour, class, religion, language, etc (noun)
18. The act of breaking a rule (noun)
19. The act of encouraging, persuading or advising someone to do something morally or legally wrong (noun)
20. A court, often one which specialises in a particular area of law (noun)
21. Basic, essential (adjective)
22. Laws and principles under which a country is governed (noun)
23. Done at random, without reason (adjective)
24. The act of keeping someone so that he / she cannot escape or enjoy freedom (noun)
25. The punishment of being made to live in another country, or another part of a country (noun)
26. Not biased or prejudiced (adjective)
27. Duty to do something (noun)

Exercise 2:

Here are Articles 11 – 20 of the Universal Declaration of Human Rights. In each article, there are between 2 and 5 spelling mistakes or wrong words. Identify and correct these words.

Article 11: (1) Everyone charged with a penal offence has the right to be presumed inocent until proved guilty according to law in a public trail at which he / she has had all the guarantees necessary for his / her defense.
(2) No one shall be held guilty of any penal offence on account of any act or omission which did not constitute a penal offence, under national or international law, at the time when it was comitted. Nor shall a heavier penaltey be imposed than the one that was applicable at the time the penal offence was committed.

Article 12: No one shall be subjected to arbitary interference with his / her privatecy, family home or correspondence, not to attacks upon his / her honour and reputeation. Everyone has the right to the projection of the law against such interference or attacks.

Article 13: (1) Everyone has the right to freedom of movement and residents within the boarders of each estate.
(2) Everyone has the right to leave any country, including his / her own, and to return to his / her country.

Article 14: (1) Everyone has the right to seek and to enjoy in other countries assylum from presecution.
(2) This right may not be inboked in the case of prossecutions genuinely arising from non-political crimes or from acts contrary to the purposes and principals of the United Nations.

Article 15: (1) Everyone has the right to a nationality.
(2) No one shall be arbitrarily depraved of his / her nationality nor denied the right to change his / her nationality.

For reference see *Dictionary of Law* 4th edition (A & C Black 0-7475-6636-4).

Article 16: (1) Men and women of full age, without any limmitation due to race, nationality or religious, have the right to marry and to found a family. They are entitled to equal rights as to marriage, during marriage, and at its dissolluttion.
(2) Marriage shall be entered into only with the free and full consend of the intending spouses.
(3) The family is the natural and fondmental group unit of society and is entitled to protection by society and state.

Article 17: (1) Everyone has the right to own property alone, as well as in asociattion with others.
(2) No one shall be abitrarily deprived of his / her property.

Article 18: Everyone has the right to freedom of thought, consience and religion: this right includes freedom to change his / her religion or believe, and freedom, either alone or in community with others and in public or private, to manifest his / her religion or belief in teaching, practise, warship and observance.

Article 19: Everyone has the right to freedom of opinion and expression: this right includes freedom to hold opinions without inteferance and to seek, receive and impart information and ideas through any media and regardless of frontears.

Article 20: (1) Everyone has the right to freedom of peaceful asembly and association.
(2) No one shall be cambelled to belong to an association.

Exercise 3:

Here is a summary of articles 21 – 30. Using your own words and ideas, explain what you think each one means. You will find a more detailed explanation of each one in the answer key at the back of this book.

Article 21: Free elections, and the right to participate in government.
Article 22: Right to social security.
Article 23: Right to desirable work and to join trade unions.
Article 24: Right to rest and leisure.
Article 25: Right to adequate living standards.
Article 26: Right to education.
Article 27:Right to participate in the cultural life of the community.
Article 28: Right to peace and order.
Article 29: Duty to preserve other people's rights and freedoms.
Article 30: Freedom from interference in all of the above rights.

Now go to *Human Rights 2* on the next page.

For reference see *Dictionary of Law* 4th edition (A & C Black 0-7475-6636-4).

In each of situations 1 – 29, one or more of the articles from the *Universal Declaration of Human Rights* has been broken or abused. Match each of the situations with the relevant article or articles (see pages 40 – 42). Choose from between Article 3 and Article 26 *only*.

1. Children between the age of 5 and 11 have to go to school, but their parents must pay for it.

2. A man has his house broken into and his television stolen. He goes to the police but they tell him to go away because they have more important things to do.

3. Archie White, a magistrate, has his car stolen. The police arrest and charge the man they think is responsible. The next day the man is taken to court for an initial hearing. The chairman of the justices (the head magistrate) in the courtroom is Archie White. He tells the members of the public that they have to leave the courtroom.

4. Staff employed by Kaput Computers have to start work at 7 in the morning and work until 7 in the evening, with only a half hour break for lunch. They work from Monday to Saturday, and do not get paid leave.

5. A couple wants to have a baby. The government says that the country is overpopulated and tells them that they cannot have a baby yet.

6. A new government tells all public servants that they have to become a member of their political party. Anyone who refuses will lose their job.

7. John Doe is arrested because the police think he has killed someone. Before his trial has begun, a popular newspaper publishes an article about him (complete with photographs of his arrest) with the headline 'Vicious murderer John Doe caught!'

8. Two friends, one white and one black, have been threatened with violence. They go to the police to ask for protection. The police agree to help the white man, but not the black man.

9. A journalist writes a newspaper article explaining why he opposes his country's foreign policy. He is told by the government that he has become *persona non grata*, he must leave the country immediately and never return.

10. A woman who lives in a capital city wants to visit her sick father, who lives 200 km away. She is told that she cannot leave the city to visit him.

11. A poor man murders someone and is sent to prison. A rich man commits a murder in similar circumstances but is allowed to go free.

12. A robber is sent to prison for 5 years. While he is in prison, the government confiscates all his belongings, and then destroys his house.

13. A man travels to another country where he asks to stay because he is frightened of remaining in his home country. He is immediately sent back to the country he came from.

14. The Republic of Istanata has never given women the right to vote.

For reference see *Dictionary of Law* 4th edition (A & C Black 0-7475-6636-4).

15. At a party, a woman tells a group of friends that she thinks the government of her country is corrupt and incompetent. The next day she is arrested and never seen again.

16. A newspaper editor dislikes a famous popular actress, so publishes an article about her. The article describes the actress as 'ugly, stupid, greedy and unable to act'.

17. A group of about 200 people hold a meeting in a public building to discuss their government's policies. The police arrive and arrest them all.

18. The government intercepts, opens and reads one of their key opponent's letters and other mail.

19. A famous political author writes a book criticising the police. She then leaves her home to go on a tour to promote her book. While she is away, the police start harassing her husband and children.

20. A husband and wife get divorced. The law in their country says that in any divorce case the man automatically gets custody of the children.

21. A woman joins a trade union. The company she works for discovers this and immediately dismisses her.

22. A man loses his job and cannot find work. His country does not offer financial support for people who are out of work.

23. A 17-year-old boy murders someone a few days before his 18th birthday. He is arrested, and six months later the case goes to court. His country has the death penalty for murder if the murderer is 18 or over. The judge sentences him to death and he is executed.

24. A policeman does not like the look of a young man sitting on a park bench, so arrests him, takes him to the police station and puts him in a police cell.

25. The police suspect that a man is a member of a terrorist organisation. They hit him, deprive him of food, water and sleep, and burn him with cigarettes until he confesses.

26. A poor man borrows money from a wealthy factory owner. He is unable to pay the money back. The factory owner takes the man's 12-year-old son and makes him work in the factory to pay off the debt.

27. A new government closes all the churches, temples, mosques and synagogues in its country, and forbids anyone from attending services there.

28. A family want to take a holiday abroad, and apply for passports. They are told that they cannot have passports and cannot go abroad.

29. Mr Smith and Ms Jones do exactly the same job for the same company. They have the same qualifications and the same experience. Mr Smith receives £35,000 a year, and Ms Jones receives £28,000 a year.

For reference see *Dictionary of Law* 4th edition (A & C Black 0-7475-6636-4).

Latin words and expressions are still relatively common in the legal profession. How many of the meanings on the left can you match with the expressions on the right?

1. By the operation of the law.	ab initio
2. Caught in the act of committing a crime.	actus reus
3. On the face of it, or as things seem at first.	ad litem
4. A gift (usually money) with no obligations attached.	bona fide(s)
5. Starting again.	bona vacantia
6. On its own, or all alone.	consensus ad idem
7. The right to be heard in a court.	corpus delicti
8. Among / In addition to other things.	de facto
9. A legal action or application pursued by one party only.	de jure
10. After the event.	de novo
11. Equally, or with no distinction.	doli capax
12. An act, such as murder, which is a crime in itself.	doli incapax
13. When a threat is implied in a contract, and as a result the contract is invalid.	ex gratia
14. A legal remedy against wrongful imprisonment.	ex parte
15. Taken as a matter of fact, even though the legal status may not be certain.	ex post facto
16. For a short time.	habeas corpus
17. Legal action against a person (for example, one party in a case claims that the other should do some act or pay damages).	in flagrante delicto
18. By this fact, or the fact itself shows this to be true.	in loco parentis
19. Acting in place of a parent.	in personam
20. A matter on which a judgement has been given.	in rem
21. A decision correctly made by a court, which can be used as a precedent.	inter alia
22. Capable of committing a crime.	in terrorem
23. The duty to prove that what has been alleged in court is true.	ipso facto
24. In total good faith, a state which should exist between parties to some types of legal relationship.	ipso jure
25. A real agreement to a contract by both parties.	locus standi
26. A situation where the legal title is clear.	mala in se
27. Referring to the case at law.	mala prohibita
28. Mad, or not completely sane.	mens rea
29. With no owner, or no obvious owner.	non compos mentis
30. The mental state required to be guilty of committing a crime.	onus probandi
31. An action done in return for something done or promised.	pari passu
32. From the beginning.	per curiam
33. Legal action against a thing (for example, one party claims property or goods in the possession of another).	per se
34. An act forbidden by criminal law.	prima facie
35. Not capable of committing a crime.	pro tempore
36. The real proof that a crime has been committed.	quid pro quo
37. An act which is not a crime, but is forbidden.	res judicata
38. In good faith.	uberrimae fidei
39. Acting in a way which exceeds your legal powers.	ultra vires

For reference see *Dictionary of Law* 4th edition (A & C Black 0-7475-6636-4).

Legal referencing

Contracts, formal letters and other legal documents frequently contain 'reference' words that are not often used in other areas of English. These words refer to time, place, result, etc, in connection with the documents they appear in.

Complete sentences 1 – 14 with appropriate words from the box. To help you, each sentence is followed by an explanation in italics of the function of the missing word.

> aforementioned   hereafter   hereby   herein   hereinafter   hereof   hereto (x2)
> heretofore   hereunder   herewith   thereafter   therein   thereinafter   thereinbefore

1. We are somewhat confused, as the contract we received named the company as The Sophos Partnership in the first paragraph, but _____ as Sophos Ltd. (*listed or mentioned afterwards in the document*)

2. Could you explain why the interest rate is quoted as 17% on the final page of the agreement you sent us, but as 15% _____. (*listed or mentioned earlier in a document*)

3. He was present when the exchange took place, and has been summoned as witness _____. (*of this event / fact*)

4. For more information, see the documents listed _____. (*below this heading or phrase*)

5. All parties are expected to comply with the conditions stated _____, unless a formal application is made to do otherwise. (*in this document*)

6. Final delivery of the merchandise is to be made no later than the dates listed _____. (*relating or belonging to this document*)

7. The copyright for this book will _____ be in the name of the author, Archibald Thrupp. (*from this time on*)

8. According to the schedule of payments attached _____, invoices must be submitted at the end of each month. (*to this document*)

9. You are advised to refer to the previous contract, and the terms and conditions cited _____. (*in that document*)

10. The accused is to report to his probationer twice a week for the first month, and _____ once a week for the next five months. (*after that*)

11. The parties _____ acting as trustees are to be consulted regularly. (*previously, earlier or before now*)

12. Thank you for the prompt despatch of our goods. Please find a cheque enclosed _____. (*together with this letter or document*)

13. This agreement is made on 1 April 2007 between Blueberry Press (_____ called the PUBLISHER), and Michael Halmsworth (_____ called the AUTHOR). (*stated later in this document: the same word should be used to complete both gaps*)

14. Mr Harrison has failed to comply with the terms set out in his contract, and we _____ revoke the contract. (*as a result or in this way*)

15. The _____ company was awarded the contract under certain conditions. (*mentioned earlier*)

For reference see *Dictionary of Law* 4th edition (A & C Black 0-7475-6636-4).

Complete the sentences and definitions below with words and expressions related to driving, and write your answers in the appropriate space in the table at the bottom of the page. The first and last letters of each word are already in the table. If you do this correctly, you will reveal a word in the shaded vertical strip that means 'a note on a driving licence to show that the holder has been convicted of a traffic offence'.

1. Driving a vehicle in such a way that it may cause damage to property or injure people, where the driver is unaware of causing a risk to other people, is called _____ driving.

2. The breaking of a rule or regulation is called a _____.

3. An offence committed when driving faster than the speed limit is called _____.

4. _____ (*2 words*) is the offence of taking a vehicle without the owner's permission, and using it to drive about (usually in a dangerous manner).

5. The minimum type of insurance required when driving a motorised vehicle is called _____ (*2 words*) insurance.

6. A person who is _____ from driving has been legally banned from driving a motorised vehicle for a certain period of time.

7. If you are stopped by the police while driving because you have done something wrong, they may offer you a _____ (*2 words*), which means that they fine you a certain amount of money and give you automatic penalty points 'on the spot'.

8. _____ is a verb which has a similar meaning *to obey*, and is often used in connection with obeying the rules of the road.

9. It is an offence to drive with _____ brakes, steering, tyres or eyesight (in other words, anything that doesn't work properly).

10. _____ (*2 words*), also called *driving with excess alcohol*, is considered to be one of the more serious road traffic offences.

11. It is an offence not to wear a _____ when driving or riding in a car.

For reference see *Dictionary of Law* 4th edition (A & C Black 0-7475-6636-4).

People in the law 1

This exercise tests your knowledge of the names we give to people who work in or for the legal system, or people who become involved in a legal process.

Complete each sentence with an appropriate word (the *first* and *last* letters have been given to you in each case), and use your answers to fill in the crossword on the next page.

Across

2.   A l_____r is a general term for any qualified member of the legal profession.

6.   An a_____y is somebody who is legally allowed to act on behalf of someone else.

11.   A member of *4 down* is called a j_____r.

12.   The j_____y is the collective word for all judges in a country, as well as the court system in general.

13.   An a_____e is somebody who has the right to speak in open court as the representative of a party in a legal case.

15.   A t_____r is a man who has made a will.

16.   A b_____r is a member of the legal profession who can plead or argue a case in one of the higher courts of law.

19.   An a_____t is a person who appeals to a higher court in order to get it to change a decision or a sentence imposed by a lower court.

20.   A c_____t is somebody who is kept in prison as punishment for a crime.

21.   The person who is elected by the other 11 members of *4 down* is called the f_____n.

23.   A p_____n officer supervises people who have committed something wrong but are not sent to prison, or people who have been released early from prison on certain conditions.

24.   A s_____t is someone whom the police believe has committed a crime.

26.   A w_____s is someone who sees something happen, or is present when it happens.

27.   A j_____e is an official who presides over a court and in civil cases decides which party is in the right.

Down

1.   A c_____t is a person who is represented by a *2 across*.

3.   A c_____t is a person who takes legal action against someone in the civil courts.

4.   A group of 12 citizens who are sworn to decide whether someone is guilty or not guilty on the basis of the evidence they hear in court is called a j_____y.

5.   Somebody who receives something under a will is called a b_____y.

7.   A m_____e is an official (who is not a *2 across* and who is usually unpaid) who tries cases in a lower court.

8.   An a_____r is somebody who decides who is right and what should be done in a disagreement or dispute.

9.   A t_____r is someone who has committed a civil wrong, or *tort*.

10.   The person who brings criminal charges against someone in a court is called a p_____r.

14.   A d_____t is someone who is sued in a civil case or somebody who is accused of a crime in a criminal case.

17.   A person who applies for a court order is called an a_____t.

18.   A s_____r is a *2 across* who has passed the examinations of the Law Society and has a valid certificate to practise, who gives advice to members of public and acts for them in legal matters.

22.   A c_____r is a public official who investigates the cause of death or the reason for it, especially if it is sudden or unexpected.

25.   C_____l is the term for a *16 across* acting for one of the parties in a legal action.

For reference see *Dictionary of Law* 4th edition (A & C Black 0-7475-6636-4).

For reference see *Dictionary of Law* 4th edition (A & C Black 0-7475-6636-4).

People in the law 2

Complete these paragraphs (which are taken from the A & C Black *Dictionary of Law*) with words or expressions from the box.

1. accused	2. adoption	3. affiliation	4. appointed	5. bench	6. biased
7. called to the Bar	8. challenged	9. clerk	10. commit	11. criminal	12. Crown Court
13. electoral register	14. eligible	15. exclusively	16. Inns of Court	17. inquests	
18. jurors	19. jury service	20. lay	21. libel	22. Magistrates' Courts	23. misconduct
24. on bail	25. Parliament	26. political	27. practise	28. pupillage	29. recorders
30. right of audience	31. sentence	32. solicitor	33. stipendiary	34. trial	35. verdict

Barristers

In England and Wales, a *barrister* is a member of one of the _____ (= the four law societies in London to which lawyers are members); he or she has passed examinations and spent one year in _____ (= training) before being _____ (= being fully accepted to practise law). Barristers have the _____ in all courts in England and Wales: in other words, they have the right to speak, but they do not have that right _____.

Magistrates

Magistrates usually work in _____. These courts hear cases of petty crime, _____, _____, maintenance and violence in the home. The court can _____ someone for _____ or for _____ in a _____. There are two main types of *magistrates*: _____ magistrates (qualified lawyers who usually sit alone); _____ *magistrates* (unqualified, who sit as a _____ of three and can only sit if there is a justices' _____ present to advise them).

Judges

In England, *judges* are _____ by the Lord Chancellor. The minimum requirement is that one should be a barrister or _____ of ten years' standing. The majority of judges are barristers, but they cannot _____ as barristers. _____ are practising barristers who act as judges on a part-time basis. The appointment of judges is not a _____ appointment, and judges remain in office unless they are found guilty of gross _____. Judges cannot be Members of _____.

The jury

Juries are used in _____ cases, and in some civil actions, notably actions for _____. They are also used in some coroner's _____. The role of the jury is to use common sense to decide if the _____ should be for or against the _____. Members of a jury (called _____) normally have no knowledge of the law and follow the explanations given to them by the judge. Anyone whose name appears on the _____ and who is between the ages of 18 and 70 is _____ for _____. Judges, magistrates, barristers and solicitors are not eligible for jury service, nor are priests, people who are _____, and people suffering from mental illness. People who are excused jury service include members of the armed forces, Members of Parliament and doctors. Potential jurors can be _____ if one of the parties to the case thinks they are or may be _____.

For reference see *Dictionary of Law* 4th edition (A & C Black 0-7475-6636-4).

Privacy and data protection

A lot of people and organisations, ranging from shops and credit card companies to government agencies, have personal data (= *details*) about us in their files and on their computers. Many people are worried that this data could be used against them or could 'fall into the wrong hands'. In Britain, the Data Protection Act sets out rules about how this data is processed and used by *data controllers* (= the people who hold details about us).

The following sentences summarise the main points of the Data Protection Act. However, each sentence contains between 1 and 4 spelling mistakes or wrong words. Identify and correct each one.

Surprisingly, there are no specific privacy laws in Britain, and people who feel they have been subjected to *unwanted intrusion* to their privacy often turn to the European Convention of Human Rights, and specifically Article 8, which concerns the right to *respect for an individual's private life*. In other cases, the United Nations Declaration of Human Rights contains a similar article (Article 12) which could be referred to. Infringements of privacy in Britain are sometimes referred to the European Court of Human Rights.

1. Data controllers should compliy with the rules of good information handling practise, known as the data protection principals.

2. Personal data should be proccesed fairly and lawfully, should be acurrate and relavant, and should be subject to appropriate secureity.

3. A person has the right to find out what infermation is held about them on computer and in some paper records. This is called the *right of supject acess*.

4. A person has the right to find out what credit agencys report about them and to be able to correct any mistakes in these reports.

5. A person has the right to prevent data being procesed if they think it is likely to cause them or anyone else unjustifried substantial damaging or substantial destress.

6. A person has the right to require the data controller not to use their personal detales to markit them with products, services or ideals.

7. A person has the right to know if a computer is used to process information about them in order to take a decisive that will effect them, and in some cases can present decisions being made about them which are based solely on automatic processing.

8. A person has the right to have unaccurate information about them ammended or destroyed.

9. A person who has suffered damage or distress as a result of a data controller failing to comply with the Data protection Act has the right to clam condensation from the data controller.

10. A person can issue court preceedings against a data controller if a sollution to any of the above points cannot be met by dealing directly with the data controller.

For reference see *Dictionary of Law* 4th edition (A & C Black 0-7475-6636-4).

Property

Test your knowledge with this quiz.

1. Rearrange the letters in **bold** to make a word: the absolute right to hold land or property for an unlimited time without paying rent is called **rofedleh**.

2. What is the difference between the answer to number 1 above, and the word *leasehold*?

3. True or false: the way in which a piece of land is held (as in 1 and 2 above) is called *land tenure*.

4. Choose the correct word in **bold** to complete this definition: a person or company which rents a house, flat or office in which to live or work is called a **tender** / **tenure** / **tenement** / **tenant** / **tentacle**.

5. In Britain, a person who arranges for the sale of property is called an *estate agent*. What is the American equivalent of this expression?

6. True or false: the transferring of property from one person to another is called *conversion*.

7. When you buy a house, why is it important to get the *title deeds* and keep them safe?

8. Imagine that you are buying a house with the help of a mortgage from the bank. The national interest rate looks likely to rise rapidly over the next year or so. Should you consider getting a *fixed-rate mortgage* or a *variable-rate mortgage*?

9. If you take out a mortgage to buy a house, and you use the house as security, the mortgage-lender might repossess (= *take back*) your house if you are unable to pay back the money. What is this called? Is it:
   (a) disclosure   (b) exposure   (c) foreclosure

10. A married couple buy a house as *joint tenants*. Who actually *owns* the house? Is it:
    (a) the husband   (b) the wife   (c) they both own it equally   (d) it depends how much each person paid towards the house.

11. The new owner of a house discovers that there is a *right of way* in his garden. What does this mean?
    (a) He can build another house in the garden if he wants.
    (b) He must sell part of the garden after a fixed period of time.
    (c) Other people can walk through his garden to get from one place to another.
    (d) Farmers can let their cows and sheep use his garden.

12. A woman is buying a house. She makes a price offer, which is accepted by the seller. She is then *gazumped*. Would she be happy or unhappy about this?

13. Choose the correct word in bold to complete this definition: a liability such as a mortgage or charge which is often attached to a property or piece of land is called an **enforcement** / **encumbrance** / **endowment** / **engrossment** / **encroachment**.

14. In Britain, house buyers must pay tax on the documents that record the purchase of the house (if the house costs more than a certain amount). What do we call this tax? Is it:
    (a) excise duty   (b) customs duty   (c) active duty   (d) double duty   (e) stamp duty

For reference see *Dictionary of Law* 4th edition (A & C Black 0-7475-6636-4).

Exercise 2:

Imagine that you want to buy a property. Below are the different stages that you will normally (and ideally) go through. Complete the gaps with words and expressions from the box.

alterations	appoint	asking	authority	balance	bound	boundaries	clauses
completion	confirmation	contract	covenants	deposit	disclose	disputes	
fees	offer	ownership	planning permission	plans	possession	preservation	
Registry	restrictions	signing	stamp	structural	survey	surveyor	title deed

1. You make an _____ on the _____ price (the price that the seller is asking for the house), which is accepted by the seller.

2. You _____ a solicitor to help you make your purchase.

3. You solicitor receives _____ of your accepted offer, and also any necessary details from the estate agent.

4. The seller's solicitor sends your solicitor a draft _____. This is checked to make sure there are no unusual _____.

5. At the same time, the seller's solicitor sends your solicitor the seller's _____. This is carefully checked for any _____ that might apply to _____ of the property. At the same time, the seller should make your solicitor aware of any problems with the property (for example, _____ with his / her neighbours, any approved or unapproved _____ that he / she has made to the property, relevant information on _____ adjoining other properties and public land, _____ or _____ orders that may restrict development of the property, whether you will need to get _____ before making changes to the property, etc).

6. If the contract is approved, copies of it are prepared for _____ by both you and the seller.

7. Before you do this, however, your solicitor should ask the local _____ (for example, the local town council) to _____ any information it has on _____ for the area around the property you are buying (for example, there may be plans to build an airport at the end of your back garden, or a motorway across your lawn at the front).

8. At the same time, you should ask for a _____ of the property by a chartered _____. He / she will tell you if there are any problems with the property (for example, rising damp, dry rot, unsound _____ features, etc).

9. If you are happy with everything, you now sign the contract: you are now legally _____ to buy the property (you cannot pull out of the agreement, unless further checks by your solicitor produce unfavourable information that has been kept secret from you; for example, he / she may discover that the property details the seller has provided are not accurate).

10. Your solicitor arranges a _____ date with the seller's solicitor – this is the date when you will take official _____ of the property – and both you and the seller exchange contracts through your solicitors. Your title deeds are prepared.

11. You pay your solicitor his _____, the money for the property (assuming you have already paid a _____ on the property, you will now need to pay the outstanding _____), the relevant _____ duty and Land _____ fees.

12. You get your copy of the deeds and the key to the front door. Congratulations, and welcome to your new home!

Punishments and penalties

Check your knowledge of punishment and penalty vocabulary with this quiz.

1. *Punish* is the verb and *punishment* is the noun, but what is the adjective form of the word? What are the verb and adjective forms of the noun *penalty*?

2. Choose the most appropriate word in **bold** in this sentence:
   'The court ordered the defendant to pay **purgative** / **punishing** / **punitive** / **pugnacious** damages to the claimant for the emotional distress he had caused.'

3. Rearrange the letters in **bold** to make words:
   'After the jury returned a 'guilty' verdict on the defendant, the judge **nopcnedoru tescenen** on him.'

4. What do we call a punishment which is considered to be strong enough to stop someone from committing a crime? Is it:
   (a) a detergent   (b) a deterrent   (c) a detriment   (d) a determinant

5. Some countries still have *corporal punishment* and some still have *capital punishment*. What happens to the people who receive these punishments?

6. In Britain, a man is stopped by the police for driving at 45 in a 30mph zone. What will (probably) happen to him?

7. Next week, the same man is stopped again, and the police discover that he has been drinking alcohol and has over twice the allowed limit of alcohol in his body. What will probably happen to him now?

8. Rearrange the letters in **bold** to make words. The *first* and *last* letters of each word are in the correct place:
   'If a defendant is found *guilty* of an offence in a court of law, he is **ciecnotvd**. If he is found *not guilty*, he is **ateqciutd**.'

9. What's the difference between a *custodial sentence*, a *suspended sentence* and *probation*?

10. A young man gets drunk and starts a fight in a bar, and as a result receives a *banning order* from a magistrate. What is he not allowed to do?

For reference see *Dictionary of Law* 4th edition (A & C Black 0-7475-6636-4).

11. The same young man has a long history of harassing and intimidating his neighbours, stealing from shops and damaging property. He receives an *ASBO* and is ordered to sign an *ABC*. What do you think these abbreviations stand for?

12. What kind of person would be sent to a *remand centre*?

13. What is the maximum penalty allowed for crime in the United Kingdom?

14. *Prison* is a noun. What is the verb form of this word?

15. A judge sends someone to prison for a period of 5 years, and tells him / her that by law they cannot be released earlier. True or false: this is called a *determinate sentence*.

16. A woman is sentenced to 6 months in prison for theft, 4 months in prison for selling drugs, and 1 month in prison for refusing to pay her council tax. The judge tells her that these sentences will be *concurrent*, or *run concurrently*. What is the maximum length of time the woman will spend in prison?

17. Rearrange the letters in **bold** to make words:
The same woman has her sentence reduced because of **dogo hevirobua** and is released after only 4 months.

18. True or false: If someone receives a *community service order*, they have to go to prison.

19. A company signs a *bond* at the same time that is signs a contract with another company. What will happen to the company if they fail to comply with the terms of the contract?

20. Choose the correct word in **bold** in this sentence:
An **injection / injunction / injury / injustice** is a court order telling someone to stop doing something, or not to do something.

21. What do we call money that is paid from one party to another to cover the cost of damage, loss, injury or hardship? (Clue: it begins with *c* and ends with *n*)

22. Mr Smith goes to the Bahamas to start a new life. While he is there, an English court applies a *freezing order* to Mr Smith's assets. Would Mr Smith be happy or unhappy about this?

For reference see *Dictionary of Law* 4th edition (A & C Black 0-7475-6636-4).

Types of court

Complete definitions 1 – 18 with words / expressions from the box. Note that several of these are related to British or English and Welsh law only, although other countries will usually have an equivalent.

- Admiralty Court
- Commercial Court
- coroner's court
- County Court
- courthouse
- court-martial
- Court of Appeal
- Court of Protection
- Crown Court
- employment tribunal
- European Court of Human Rights
- European Court of Justice
- High Court
- House of Lords
- Lands Tribunal
- magistrates' court
- rent tribunal
- small claims court

1. A _____ is a court that deals with disputes over small amounts of money.

2. A _____ is a civil or criminal court to which a person may go to ask for an award or sentence to be changed.

3. A _____ is a court which tries someone serving in the armed forces for offences against military discipline.

4. A _____ is the general word for a building in which trials take place.

5. A _____ is one of the types of court in England and Wales which hears local civil cases.

6. The _____ is a court which considers the rights of citizens of states which are parties to the European Convention for the Protection of Human Rights.

7. An _____ is a body responsible for hearing work-related complaints as specified by statute.

8. A _____ is a court which hears cases of petty crime, adoption, affiliation, maintenance and violence in the home (= *domestic violence*), and which can also commit someone for trial or sentencing in a Crown Court.

9. A _____ is a court presided over by a public official (usually a doctor or lawyer) who investigates sudden, unexpected and violent deaths.

10. A _____ is a court above the level of a magistrates' court which hears criminal cases.

11. A _____ is a court which deals with compensation claims relating to land.

12. A _____ is a court in the Queen's Bench Division (= one of the main divisions of the High Court) which hears cases relating to business disputes.

For reference see *Dictionary of Law* 4th edition (A & C Black 0-7475-6636-4).

13.   A _____ is a court which adjudicates in disputes about money paid or services provided in return for borrowing something – usually buildings or land.

14.   The _____ is the main civil court in England and Wales.

15.   The _____ is the court set up to see that the principles of law as laid out in the Treaty of Rome are observed and applied correctly in the European Union.

16.   A _____ is a court appointed to serve the interests of people who are not capable of dealing with their own affairs, such as patients who are mentally ill.

17.   The _____ is court which is part of the Queen's Bench Division (see number 12 above), which decides in disputes involving ships.

18.   The _____ is the highest court of appeal in the United Kingdom (although appellants unhappy with a decision made here can appeal to the European Court of Justice).

Exercise 2:

Decide which of the courts above is most likely to deal with the following situations.

1.   *HMS Decrepit* and *HMS Leaky* collide during exercises in the North Sea. The captains of both vessels blame each other.

2.   Mr Johnson and Mrs Johnson are getting divorced. Mrs Johnson demands to have the house, the car, 75% of Mr Johnson's life savings and their pet cat, Tigger. "No way!" says an angry Mr Johnson.

3.   One evening, Mr Waring goes to his favourite seafood restaurant for dinner. The next morning he is found dead in bed.

4.   Two separate companies, *English International Telecommunications* and *Britphone*, both bring out a new mobile phone which they call the '*Smell-O-Phone*'. Both companies claim that the name was their own idea.

5.   Five workers have been sacked from the computer manufacturing company 'Compucrash' for incompetence. They believe that they have been unfairly dismissed.

6.   Mr Cassington is 98 years old and going deaf and senile. The local Social Services believe he should be put in a special home. Mr Cassington refuses to leave his own house.

7.   Mr and Mrs Waugh had a new window installed in their house. The window company now wants the Waughs to pay, but Mr Waugh is refusing because he thinks the quality of workmanship is poor.

8.   Jamie Yarnton pays £500 a month to live in Mrs Witney's house. Suddenly, Mrs Witney asks him for £1,000 a month instead. Mr Yarnton thinks this is completely unreasonable.

9.   Newspaper editor Mr Hislop publishes an article describing the Prime Minister as a 'useless, incompetent fool who can barely tie his own shoelaces, let alone run the country'. The PM decides to take immediate legal action against the paper.

10.   Corporal Jones ignored Sergeant Wilson's orders, then went 'absent without leave' for two weeks.

For reference see *Dictionary of Law* 4th edition (A & C Black 0-7475-6636-4).

Wills

Complete definitions and explanations 1 – 15 below with words and expressions from the box.

administrator	benefactor	beneficiary	codicil	deceased	dependants
estate	executor	inherit	inheritance	intestate	living wills	of age
of sound mind	power of attorney	probate	testament	trust	trustee

1. A will is often also known in legal terms as a *last will and* _____.

2. When someone makes a will, they must be _____ (in other words, they must be mentally healthy), and must be _____ (ie, over 18 in Britain)

3. When a person is making a will, their first concern is usually for their _____ (the people who he / she supports financially, for example, his / her children).

4. A person who has died recently is often referred to as the _____.

5. Someone who dies without making a will is said to have died _____.

6. _____ is the legal acceptance that a document, and especially a will, is valid.

7. If a person dies without making a will, a person known as an _____ might be appointed by a court to represent the deceased.

8. A _____ is a document which makes a change or an addition to a will.

9. A person who is appointed by a person making his / her will to make sure that the terms of the will are carried out is called an _____.

10. A person who gives property or money to others in a will is called a _____, and the person who is left money or property in a will is called a _____.

11. The money and property that is owned by a person, especially someone who has died, is known as an _____.

12. _____ is a verb which means 'to acquire something from a person who has died'. The property which is received is called an _____.

13. Money or property which is looked after for someone by someone else (for example, money which has been left in a will that someone will receive when they reach a particular age) is called a _____. The person who looks after this money is called a _____.

14. People who are seriously ill often appoint someone to deal with their affairs for them. This is called _____.

15. Many people now write special healthcare directives called _____, which indicate how they want to be treated if they become seriously ill.

For reference see *Dictionary of Law* 4th edition (A & C Black 0-7475-6636-4).

Complete each gap below with <u>one</u> word that can be used with the words and expressions in *italics*. All of these words, when used together with the italicised words, are connected directly or indirectly with different aspects of law (criminal, business, commercial, property, etc). The first letter of each word is already there for you, the function of each word is explained in brackets after each gap, and the first one has been done as an example.

1.   This a____ (*adjective*) can come <u>before</u> *discharge, majority, monopoly, privilege, right* and *title*. (Answer = **absolute**)

2.   This a____ (*verb / noun*) can come <u>before</u> the words *your authority, of power, of process* and *of human rights*.

3.   This a____ (*noun*) can come <u>before</u> the expressions *in personam, in rem* and *in tort*, and <u>after</u> the expression *to take legal*.

4.   This a____ (*adjective*) can come <u>before</u> *outcome, party, possession* and *witness*.

5.   This a____ (*noun*) can come <u>before</u> *agreement, award, board* and *clause*, and also <u>after</u> the expressions *to submit a dispute to, to refer a question to, to take a dispute to* and *to go to*.

6.   This b____ (*noun*) can come <u>before</u> the expressions *of confidence, of contract, of promise, of the peace, of trust* and *of warranty*, and <u>between</u> the prepositions *in + of*.

7.   This c____ (*noun*) can come <u>before</u> *allowance, assets, crime, expenditure, gains, goods, levy, loss* and *punishment*, and in the expression *to make political ___ out of something*.

8.   This c____ (*noun*) can come <u>before</u> the expressions *of approval, of deposit, of incorporation, of judgement, of origin, of registration, of registry* and *of service*.

9.   This c____ (*adjective*) can come <u>before</u> the words *action, court, disobedience, disorder, law, liberties, rights* and *strife*.

10.   This c____ (*adjective*) can come <u>before</u> the words *assault, carrier, land, law, ownership, position, pricing* and *seal*, and <u>after</u> the expression *tenancy in*.

11.   This c____ (*noun*) can come <u>before</u> the words *fund, order*, and *package*, and <u>before</u> the expressions *for damage, for loss of office* and *for loss of earnings*.

12.   This c____ (*noun*) can come <u>before</u> the words *confidence, council, credit, goods, group, legislation* and *protection*.

13.   This c____ (*noun*) can come <u>before</u> the words *law, note* and *work*, <u>before</u> the expressions *of employment, of service* and *under seal*, <u>after</u> the word *under*, and <u>after</u> the expressions *by private* and *to void a*.

14.   This c____ (*noun*) can come <u>before</u> the words *action, case* and *order*, <u>before</u> the expressions *of appeal, of first instance, of last resort* and *of law*, <u>after</u> the words *open, criminal* and *civil*, and <u>after</u> the expressions *out of* and *to take someone to*.

15.   This c____ (*noun*) can come <u>before</u> the words *act, action, bankruptcy, court, damage, law, libel, negligence, offence, record* and *responsibility*, and <u>after</u> the words *hardened* and *habitual*.

For reference see *Dictionary of Law* 4th edition (A & C Black 0-7475-6636-4).

16. This c____ (*noun*) can come <u>before</u> the words *barrier, clearance, declaration, duty, examination, formalities, officer, seal, tariffs* and *union,* <u>before</u> the expression *and Excise,* and <u>after</u> the expression *to go through.*

17. This d____ (*noun*) can come <u>before</u> the words *counsel, statement* and *witness,* <u>before</u> the expression *before claim* and <u>after</u> the expression *to file a.*

18. This d____ (*noun*) can come <u>before</u> the words *abuse, addict, addiction, baron, czar, dealer, runner, squad* and *trafficking,* and <u>after</u> the classification expressions *Class A, Class B* and *Class C.*

19. This f____ (*adjective*) can come *before* the words *conveyance, misrepresentation, preference, trading* and *transaction.*

20. This f____ (*noun*) can come <u>before</u> the expressions *of assembly, of association, of information, of movement, of speech, of the press* and *of thought, conscience and religion.*

21. This i____ (*noun*) can come <u>before</u> the words *documents, papers, parade* and *theft,* <u>after</u> the word *false,* and <u>after</u> the expressions *to change your, to be asked for proof of* and *a case of mistaken.*

22. This i____ (*adjective*) can be used <u>before</u> the words *contract, malice, term* and *trust,* and <u>before</u> the expression *terms and conditions.*

23. This i____ (*adjective*) can be used <u>before</u> the words *accident, development, dispute, espionage, injury, property, relations* and *tribunal,* and <u>before</u> the expression *arbitration tribunal.*

24. This j____ (*adjective*) can be used <u>before</u> the words *account, beneficiary, committee, discussions, heir, liability, management, owner, ownership, signatory, tenancy* and *tortfeasors,* and <u>before</u> the expressions *and several, and several liability* and *commission of inquiry.*

25. This j____ (*noun*) can be used <u>before</u> the words *creditor, debtor* and *summons,* <u>before</u> the expression *by default,* <u>after</u> the expressions *to pronounce, to enter* and *to take,* and in the expression *to give your ...on something.*

26. This j____ (*adjective*) can come <u>before</u> the words *immunity, notice, precedent, processes, review* and *separation.* In Britain, it can come <u>before</u> the expressions *Committee of the House of Lords* and *Committee of the Privy Council.*

27. This j____ (*noun*) can come <u>before</u> the words *box, room, service* and *vetting,* <u>after</u> the expression *foreman of the,* and in the expression *to be called for ... service.*

28. This l____ (*noun*) can come <u>before</u> the expressions *before action, of acknowledgement, of allotment, of application, of appointment, of attorney, of complaint, of credit, of demand, of indemnity, of intent, of reference, of renunciation* and *of request.*

29. This l____ (*adjective*) can come <u>before</u> the words *liability, market, partner, partnership* and *warranty,* and <u>before</u> the expression *liability company.*

30. This n____ (*adjective*) can come <u>before</u> the words *earnings, estate, gain, price, profit, result* and *worth.*

For reference see *Dictionary of Law* 4th edition (A & C Black 0-7475-6636-4).

How many of the words and expressions in the box can you match with words 1 – 15 in the table to make complete expressions? The first one has been done for you. Note that some of the words / expressions in the box can be matched with more than one word in the table.

```
...account   ...action   ...agent   ...allowances   ...assets   ...authority   ...bail   ...channels
   ...chattels   ...client   ...company   ...conduct   ...constable   ...copy   ...court   ...credit
     ...damages   ...defect   ...deposits   ...detective   ...directions   ...discussion   ...effects
...-ended   ...estate   ...examiner   ...force   ...hearing   ...holder   ...income   ...indorsement
      ...injury   ...inquiries   ...inspector   ...investigation   ...land   ...law   ...mediator
   ...nuisance   ...number   ...of abode   ...of advancement   ...of affairs   ...of allegiance
 ...of allocation   ...of amends   ...of appeal   ...of appointment   ...of attorney   ...of audience
 ...of case   ...of claim   ...of dishonour   of establishment   ...office   ...officer   ...of motion
...of opposition   ...of re-entry   ...of reply   ...of search   ...of service   ...of silence   ...of truth
 ...of value   ...of way   ...ownership   ...pending   ...politics   price...   ...prison   ...property
     ...proprietor   ...prosecution   ...protection   ...Receiver   ...referee   ...reference
  ...representative   ...return   ...rights   ...ruling   ...secret   ...Solicitor   ...specification
     to administer an...   to be open for...   to be open to...   to be under...   ...to buy
     to make a...   to make a false...   ...to quit   to register a...   ...to reside   ...to sell
                 to take the...   ...trade mark   ...user   ...verdict
```

1	notice: *notice of allocation, notice of appeal, notice of dishonour, notice of motion, notice of opposition, notice of service, notice to quit*
2	oath:
3	offer:
4	official:
5	open:
6	patent:
7	personal:
8	police:
9	power:
10	preliminary:
11	private:
12	registered:
13	right:
14	special:
15	statement:

Can you explain what each of these expressions means? If you are not sure, refer to the A & C Black *Dictionary of Law*, where you will find concise definitions of each one.

For reference see *Dictionary of Law* 4th edition (A & C Black 0-7475-6636-4).

Word association 3

Complete the following sentences and definitions with words that work (*collocate*) with the other words and expressions in **bold**. These all use *law* or *legal*. Where a sample sentence is given, the definition is in *italics* at the end of the sentence. Use your answers to complete the crossword on the next page. To make it more challenging for you, there are no numbers in the crossword grid, and the sentences below are in no particular order. However, we have included the first letter of each word in the grid.

1.   _____ **Law** is one of the most popular subjects on this course. (*laws relating to agreements*)

2.   The company promised to **act** _____ **the law**. (*obey the laws of a country*)

3.   Insider dealing is _____ **the law**. (*not according to the laws of a country*)

4.   You are _____ **the law** if you try to export goods without a licence. (*to do something that is not legal*)

5.   Following the assassination of the President, there was a breakdown of **law and** _____. (*a situation where the law is being obeyed by most people*)

6.   Most people in this country are **law-**_____, although there are always a few exceptions. (*respectful of the law, obeying it*)

7.   For some reason, some people seem to think they are _____ **the law**. (*do not have to obey the law*)

8.   There are two sources of law in Britain: the laws that are made in Parliament, and _____ **law**. (*law established n the basis of decisions by the court rather than by statute*)

9.   The manager **laid** _____ **the law**, and threatened to dismiss anyone who broke the regulations. (*tell someone strongly and often in an angry way what they should do: an informal expression*)

10.   Some people take **the law into their own** _____ because they do not believe the judicial system works effectively. (*to punish someone yourself without using the proper legal process: an informal expression*)

11.   Anyone who wants to run a successful business is advised to learn about _____ **law**. (*law regarding the conduct of businesses*)

12.   **Law** _____ is the activity of making sure that laws are obeyed.

13.   Any action which is permitted by the law is known as a **lawful** _____.

14.   I've lived with my partner for about 10 years, so that makes her my _____**-law wife**. (*somebody who lives with another person as a wife, although they are not legally married*)

15.   The branch of law dealing with the rights of ownership is call _____ **law**.

16.   **Law of** _____ is the law relating to how property shall pass to others when the owner dies.

17.   The continuing process of revising laws to make then better suited to the needs of society is called **law** _____.

18.   When his uncle died, Alan made a **legal** _____ on his property. (*a statement that someone owns something legally*)

For reference see *Dictionary of Law* 4th edition (A & C Black 0-7475-6636-4).

19. When he broke the contract, the company started **legal** _____ against him. (*to sue someone, to take them to court*)

20. Some people are reluctant to hire a lawyer because they can't afford the **legal** _____. (*the money spent on fees to lawyers*)

21. The office employees seven solicitors and a **legal** _____. (*a clerk in a solicitor's office who is not a solicitor and is nor articled to become one, but has passed certain exams*)

22. In some countries, people who cannot afford a lawyer may be entitled to **legal** _____. (*money that a government gives to someone to help them pay for a lawyer*)

23. Sterling is the only **legal** _____ in the United Kingdom, although some larger establishments will accept US dollars and the euro. (*money that can officially be used in a country*)

24. Mr and Mrs Thomas have been granted a **legal** _____. (*a court decree acknowledging that a married couple no longer live together but are not yet divorced*)

25. These papers are valid in your country, but unfortunately they have no **legal** _____ here. (*the official legal position of a person, company, document, etc*)

For reference see *Dictionary of Law* 4th edition (A & C Black 0-7475-6636-4).

Vocabulary record sheet

Photocopy this page as many times as you like, and use it to keep a record of new words and expressions that you learn. Try to build up your own vocabulary bank, and keep this in a file or folder with the words / expressions stored in alphabetical order for quick and easy reference. Review the items that you have recorded on a regular basis. See the next page for a model record sheet showing an example of how a vocabulary item has been recorded.

Word or expression:	
Area(s) of law (if relevant):	
Definition(s):	
Translation or equivalent in your language:	
Other forms of this word (if relevant):	
Sample sentences:	
Other collocations:	
Related words and expressions:	

Other information:

You may photocopy this page

For reference see *Dictionary of Law* 4th edition (A & C Black 0-7475-6636-4).

Vocabulary record sheet sample

This is a sample of a completed vocabulary sheet, based on the word 'copyright'. The student has included as much information about the word as possible, including its grammatical function and pronunciation. Much of the information has been taken or adapted from the A & C Black *Dictionary of Law*, a useful source of legal vocabulary.

Word or expression:	copyright (noun)
Area(s) of law (if relevant):	Intellectual property
Definition(s):	An author's legal right to publish his or her own work and not to have it copied. Also the similar right of an artist, film maker or musician.
Translation or equivalent in your language:	droits d'auteur
Other forms of this word (if relevant):	copyrighted (adjective) copyright (adjective) to copyright (verb; regular)
Sample sentences:	This work is out of copyright. The work is still in copyright. The program is protected by copyright. This article is an infringement / a breach of the author's copyright. The use of copyrighted material must be approved in advance.
Other collocations:	copyright deposit, copyright holder, copyright law, copyright notice assert your copyright
Related words and expressions:	patent, (registered) trademark, author, artist, artiste, protect, protected

Other information:

Copyright exists in original written works, in works of art and works of music. It covers films, broadcasts, recordings, etc. It also covers the layout of books, newspapers and magazines.

Copyright only exists if the work is created by a person who is qualified to hold a copyright, and is published in a country which is qualified to hold a copyright.

Copyright lasts for 50 years after the author's death (according to the Berne Convention) and for 25 years according to the Universal Copyright Convention. The European Union has adopted a copyright term of 70 years after the author's death.

Copyrighted material has to include the symbol '©', the name of the copyright holder and the date of first publication.

Do not confuse 'copyright' with 'copywriter'.

You may photocopy this page

For reference see *Dictionary of Law* 4th edition (A & C Black 0-7475-6636-4).

Answers

Before you begin: Essential words (page 1)

1. damages   2. commit   3. judicial   4. innocent   5. offence   6. lawyer   7. dispute   8. tribunal   9. case   10. judge
11. plead   12. defendant   13. claimant   14. settlement   15. arrest   16. hearing   17. convict   18. breach
19. prosecute   20. appeal   21. accuse   22. binding   23. civil   24. defence   25. contract   26. criminal   27. jury
28. evidence   29. fine   30. injunction

Remember that many of these words can have more than one meaning. To check the other meanings, refer to the A & C Black *Dictionary of Law*.

Business law 1: Key adjectives (pages 2 – 3)

Exercise 1:
1. accountable   2. ✔   3. impartial   4. intangible   5. pecuniary   6. ✔   7. void (if a contract is *void*, or *null and void*, it becomes legally *unenforceable*)   8. admissible   9. unanimous   10. eligible   11. irreconcilable   12. gross (*gross* can also mean *before tax and other deductions*: for example, *gross earnings, gross salary*, etc)   13. ✔   14. ✔ (note that a company or organisation becomes *insolvent*, a person becomes *bankrupt*)   15. fiduciary

Exercise 2:
1. occupational   2. mandatory   3. exempt   4. negotiable   5. verbatim   6. unconditional   7. fraudulent   8. feasible
9. redundant   10. Habitual   11. solvent   12. material   13. nominal   14. corporate   15. open-ended   16. litigious (the verb is *to litigate*, the noun is *litigation*. A person who litigates is a *litigant*. A lawyer who specialises in litigation is known as a *litigation practitioner*)

Business law 2: Key nouns (pages 4 – 5)

1. nominee (from the verb to *nominate*. *Nominee* can precede words such as *account* and *shareholder*: a *nominee account*; a *nominee shareholder*)   2. franchise (a *franchisee* is a person who runs a franchise, a *franchiser / franchisor* is somebody who licenses a franchise. The act of selling a licence to trade as a franchise is *franchising*: *He runs his sandwich-making chain as a franchising operation*)   3. ombudsman   4. guarantor (sometimes used in the expression *to stand guarantor for somebody*, meaning *to pay or promise to pay someone's debts*)   5. breach (common collocations of this word include: *a breach of confidence, a breach of contract, a breach of promise, a breach of the peace, a breach of trust, a breach of warranty*. It is also used with *in + of: We are in breach of Community law; The defendant is in breach of his statutory duty*, etc)   6. acceptance (someone who accepts an offer is an *acceptor*)   7. perjury (also used as a reflexive verb: *to perjure yourself*)   8. tortfeasor (from *tort*, a civil wrong. A case by a claimant who alleges he or she has suffered damage or harm is called *action in tort*)   9. compensation (from the verb *to compensate*. Compensation in this context is sometimes called *compensatory damages*)   10. mediation (from the verb *to mediate*. A person who mediates is a *mediator*)   11. debenture (collocations of this word include: *debenture register, debenture bond, debenture capital, debenture holder, debenture issue*)   12. liquidation (from the verb *to liquidate*. Often used in the expression *to go into liquidation*: *The company went into liquidation when it was declared insolvent*)   13. damages (a person or a company can *bring an action for damages* against another person or company)   14. liability (you can *accept, admit* or *refuse* liability for something. A company's *articles of association* should include a *liability clause*, which states that the liability of its members is limited. The liability of an employer for acts committed by an employee during the course of work is called *vicarious liability*)   15. negligence (from the verb *to neglect*. The adjective is *negligent*)   16. goodwill (for example, *She paid £10,000 for the goodwill of the shop, and £4,000 for the stock. Goodwill* is one of a company's intangible assets, and so is not shown in the company's accounts, unless it figures as part of the purchase price paid when acquiring another company)   17. injunction (note that some injunctions are granted temporarily until the case comes up in court. These are called *temporary* or *interlocutory injunctions*)

The word in the shaded vertical strip is *misrepresentation*.

Business law 3: Key verbs (pages 6 – 8)

Across:
3. indemnify (this is similar to *compensate*)   4. undertakes (noun = *undertaking*)   10. adjudicate (noun = *adjudication*. A person who adjudicates is an *adjudicator*)   12. liquidate (this word also means *to close down a company and sell its assets*. The noun is *liquidation*)   14. entitled (noun = *entitlement*)   15. mediate (noun = *mediation*. A person who mediates is a *mediator*)   17. drafted (noun = *draft*)   19. appointed (noun = *appointment*)   20. elapse   21. defraud   26. disclose (noun = *disclosure*)   28. banned (noun = *ban*)   29. invalidated   31. waive   32. granted (noun = *grant*)

Down:
1. ratified (noun = *ratification*)   2. blacklisted (noun = *blacklist*)   5. default   6. foreclosed (noun = *foreclosure*)   7. disputing (noun = *dispute*)   8. awarded (noun = *award*)   9. subcontracted   11. infringed (a *copyright* can also be infringed. The noun is *infringement*)   13. certified   16. exempted (noun = *exemption*)   18. wound up (noun = *winding up*)   19. alleged (note that *alleges* will not fit because of 26 across. Noun = *allegation*)   22. abide by   23. vested (also used as an adjective in expressions such as *vested interest, vested remainder*, etc)   24. claiming (noun = *claim*)   25. seek   27. strike (noun = *strike*)   30. lets (noun = *let*)

Business law 4: Key expressions (pages 9 – 10)

1. power of attorney (other expressions with *power* include: *power of advancement, power of appointment; power of search*)   2. data protection   3. without prejudice   4. joint venture   5. force majeure   6. grievance procedure
7. articles of association (also called *articles of incorporation*. A partnership has *articles of partnership*)   8. pre-emption clause (the shareholders have *pre-emption rights*)   9. winding up   10. employers' liability   11. vicarious liability
12. limited liability   13. memorandum of association   14. memorandum of satisfaction (the plural of memorandum is *memoranda*)   15. joint and several   16. out of court (for example, *a settlement was reached out of court*)
17. freezing injunction (also called a *freezing order*, and previously known as a *Mareva injunction*)   18. unliquidated damages   19. burden of proof (*to discharge a burden of proof* is the expression that is used when something that has been alleged in court is found to be true. When the prosecution must prove that what it alleges is true, we can say that

the burden of proof is on the prosecution)   20. unprofessional conduct (do not confuse this with *unreasonable conduct*, which is behaviour by a spouse which is not reasonable and shows that a marriage has broken down)   21. confidential information   22. employment tribunal (also called an *industrial tribunal*)   23. obligation of confidentiality   24. trade mark (sometimes written as one word, *trademark*. The action of trying to sell goods by giving the impression that they have been made by someone else, using that person's reputation and / or trade mark, is called *passing off*)   25. intellectual property   26. terms and conditions   27. wrongful dismissal (compare this with *unfair dismissal*, the act of removing someone from a job in a way that appears not to be reasonable, such as dismissing someone who wants to join a union)   28. unfair competition   29. fundamental breach   30. compulsory liquidation

Consumer rights (pages 11 – 12)

Here are the completed paragraphs:

Exercise 1:

Providers of goods and services (including credit providers and hire companies) all have **responsibilities and liabilities** towards the customer which are aimed at protecting the customer and his / her rights.

When you buy goods, they must be of **satisfactory quality**: the condition they are in should match your expectations based on the price you paid. They should also be '**as described**' (in other words, they must match the description made by the provider and / or the manufacturer), and they must be '**fit for purpose**' (they should do what you expect them to do).

All goods must carry a **guarantee or warranty** in case they go wrong or do not meet your expectations.

If you need to return goods to a shop or other supplier, you should do so **within a reasonable time**: many shops and suppliers specify their own limit, usually 28 days, and can refuse to do anything if there is evidence of unreasonable **wear and tear** (signs that the goods have been used more than is normal or for a purpose for which they were not designed).

If you take goods back to a shop, they are entitled to ask for **proof of purchase**, such as a **receipt**, a credit card slip, etc, that shows you actually bought the goods from them.

Many shops may refuse (illegally, if the product you have bought is faulty or **defective**) to **give a refund**, and instead of returning your money will offer you a **credit voucher** to use in that shop at a later date.

Where goods or services are ordered on the Internet, on-line shops should offer their customers a **cooling-off period** after they have ordered them, in case the customer decides to suddenly cancel their order.

On-line shops should give the customer an **accurate description** of the goods being sold, and clearly state the price, **delivery arrangements** and options (how and when the customer can expect to receive their goods, whether there is an extra charge for postage, etc).

On-line shops should also protect customers against **credit card fraud**, and should allow customers to **opt out of** receiving further information and **unsolicited telemarketing, unsolicited mail** or unsolicited email. They should also send the customer **written confirmation** of their order (often in the form of an email sent after the order has been placed).

Exercise 2:

If a service is being provided (for example, a mobile phone contract), and there is a **specified period** for the contract, this must be clearly stated by the provider.

If you buy faulty goods with a credit card, and those goods cost over £100, you have an equal **claim for compensation** against the seller of the goods and the credit card company.

Where a service such as the repair of a car is being provided, it should be done with **reasonable care and skill** (an unsatisfactory standard of work or general **poor workmanship** should *not* be accepted by the customer) for a **reasonable charge** (the customer should not have to pay an excessive amount of money) and within a reasonable time.

If you need to make a claim against a shop, company or other provider, because you have not received satisfaction from that shop, company, etc, you can do so through the **County Court**. For claims of less than £5,000, the **Small Claims** procedure should be useful.

The process is very simple: after completing a **claim form**, you ask the court to **issue the proceedings**. The court then **serves the claim** on the company or other provider. Assuming the company responds within the specified time limit, there will be a **preliminary hearing**. Later, there will be a main hearing where hopefully the judge will decide **in your favour**.

Contracts 1 (pages 13 – 14)

Exercise 1. Here is the complete text:
A contract can be defined as 'an **agreement** between two or more parties to create legal **obligations** between them'. Some contracts are made '**under seal**': in other words, they are **signed** and sealed (stamped) by the parties involved). Most contracts are made **verbally** or in **writing**. The essential elements of a contract are: (a) that an **offer** made by one party should be **accepted** by the other; (b) **consideration** (the price in money, goods or some other **reward**, paid by one party in exchange for another party agreeing to do something); (c) the **intention** to create legal relations. The **terms** of a contract may be **express** (clearly stated) or **implied** (not clearly **stated** in the contract, but generally understood). A **breach** of contract by one party of their **contractual liability** entitles the other party to **sue** for **damages** or, in some cases, to seek specific performance. In such circumstances, the contract may be **voided** (in other words, it becomes *invalid*).

Exercise 2:
1. an unspoken *implied* or *understood* contract between a shop and a customer (yes, it *is* a contract!)   2. a verbal contract

For reference see *Dictionary of Law* 4th edition (A & C Black 0-7475-6636-4).

Answers *(cont.)*

that has gone through the *offer, acceptance* and *consideration* stages.   3. a tenancy (agreement) (*pcm = per calendar month*)   4. franchise agreement (between a *franchiser* – the people who license a franchise – and a *franchisee* – the people who run the franchise)   5. loan agreement (*APR = annual percentage rate*; the *interest* that has to be paid)   6. employment contract (full-time)   7. terms and conditions of sale (purchase agreement)   8. car hire agreement

Contracts 2 (pages 15 – 16)

1. 1. part = parties   2. False. A contract which is binding must be followed exactly, unless both parties agree on a *novation* (= a transaction in which a new contract is agreed)   3. obey *and* honour
2. 1. terminator = termination   2. True   3. obligated / required
3. 1. un-negotiable = non-negotiable   2. True (it might be possible to *amend* some of the details, or make *amendments*)   3. oral / spoken
4. 1. in beach of = in breach of   2. abide by (in paragraph 1)   3. False (they breached one part, or *clause*)   4. A consideration
5. 1. period of notification = period of notice   2. agreement   3. No, it is part of a fixed-term (in his case, 18 months) contract   4. True (in other words, if either party cancels the contract early, they will still have to honour the terms of the contract for 3 months, unless there was less than 3 months to run on the contract)
6. 1. anointment = appointment   2. False (they *amalgamated*, or *joined with*, Berryhill Books)   3. False (he cannot buy more than 50% of the company's shares – a controlling interest – otherwise he will be able to decide how the company is run)   4. None (he can have no *professional dealings* with *third parties*, i.e. companies other than AKL Publishing)

Corporate responsibility 1: The environment (page 17)

Here is the completed text:
A company should ensure that its actions do not damage local and global **ecosystems**. It needs to **reduce** its use of natural **resources** such as oil, gas and other fossil fuels, and regulate its **effect** on aspects such as **climate** change, and air, sea and noise **pollution**. It needs to be aware of the dangers it might pose in terms of **ecological degradation**, and must follow local, national and international **codes**, rules, **regulations** and **protocols** designed to minimise damage . Where possible, it should **exploit** the availability of **alternative** power sources such as solar and tidal power. If the company is involved in the agricultural sector, it should support and encourage **sustainable** agriculture and forest use. If a company wishes to develop **genetically** modified products, it should do so only if it is safe, and only after public **consultation**, and it should take all necessary **precautions**. It should also have the approval of local people who might be **affected**. If accidents occur or **regulatory** breaches are made, the company must be honest and **transparent** in its dealings with those who are affected, and assist them in **implementing** procedures to reduce its **impact**.

A company that **extracts** and exploits natural **non-renewable** resources such as coal, oil or gas, or **renewable** resources such as hydro-electric power, should ensure that it avoids **conflict** with local people, and that the **human rights** of those people are not **abused** through its actions, either directly or **indirectly**. It needs to be aware of its role in **sustaining** the environment, and helping to preserve the survival of local and national **communities** (including **indigenous** people who might be less able to represent or defend themselves). A company should avoid working in or around vulnerable and **non-sustainable** communities unless its actions directly **benefit** those communities. Where people are asked to move in order for a company to exploit local resources, they should do so **voluntarily**, and should be offered adequate **compensation** for their land and **assets** (the resource being exploited should be considered as one of these).

Corporate responsibility 2: Communities (page 18)

Here is the completed text:
A company should **respect**, **protect** and **promote** national and international human rights **treaties**, **principles** and standards, regardless of whether or not these have been **ratified** by the host state, and regardless of whether or not such standards are legally-**binding** in the host state. All companies should **regulate** their behaviour accordingly. A company should respect the political **jurisdiction** of the host state, but where there are gross human rights **violations** by the government of the host state, the company should withdraw its operations from that state.

A company should **comply** with internationally-recognised labour, health, safety and **environmental** standards. It should be **committed** to ensuring that the communities it deals with and the people it employs are **treated** with **respect**. It should recognise that its operations will have a **social**, **economic** and environmental **impact** on local communities, and it should **involve** the community in any major **decision**-making process. It should **contribute** to the **development** of that community, the **preservation** of local cultures, the development of social, educational and medical **facilities** and the **sustainability** of the local economy. It should at all times **incorporate** the best **interests** of the community into its methods of operation, and actively encourage the **participation** of the community in its operations.

If a company produces essential food or medical items to sell locally, it should **implement** a policy of price **restraint** so that these products are **affordable**. It should not charge grossly **inflated** prices. If the essential products it makes carry a **patent** the company should not **enforce** this if doing so will have an **adverse** effect on the health and wellbeing of local people.

A company should not **discriminate** against, or **denigrate**, local communities or individuals on the basis of race, **gender**, culture, **ethnicity**, religion, class, **sexual orientation** or disability.

A company should display **integrity** and **transparency** in *all* its operations at *all* times.

Corporate responsibility 3: Employment (pages 19 – 20)

1. O   2. I + N   3. L   4. H   5. G   6. A + B   7. J   8. E   9. M   10. F   11. R   12. C   13. Q   14. D   15. I   16. P   17. K

Corporate responsibility 4: Financial and ethical integrity (pages 21 – 22)

Paragraph 1: 1. undermine   2. stakeholders   3. transparent   4. shareholders   5. transactions   6. solicit   7. incentive   8. bribes   9. integrity
Paragraph 2: social = socially, investing = investments, diligent = diligence, adversity = adverse, affect = effect, right =

For reference see *Dictionary of Law* 4th edition (A & C Black 0-7475-6636-4).

rights, disclosure = disclose
Paragraph 3: suspects, criminal, suspicions, authorities, barriers
Paragraph 4: A company that lends money should avoid **predatory** practices such as very high **interest rates** and short **repayment** periods, especially in situations where people are particularly financially **disadvantaged**, and it should **ensure** that its lending **policies** are **equitable**, even if this means that they have to reduce their **profit margins**.
Paragraph 5: infrange = infringe, permision = permission, acknoledgement = acknowledgement, copywrite = copyright, patient = patent, tradmark = trademark, registreed = registered, createive = creative, intelectual = intellectual, propperty = property
Paragraph 6: privacy = private, harassment = harass, intimidation = intimidating, invasion = invade, maintaining = maintenance, public = publicise, neighbours = neighbourly
Paragraph 7: Suggested answers: *Corporate governance* = the way a company behaves and the way it operates within a set of self-imposed rules, or externally-imposed legislation; *codes of conduct* = rules that determine how a company and its employees behave, dress, deal with the public, etc; *codes of best practice* = ethical and moral standards that a company imposes on itself so that it operates to the best of its ability with minimum negative effect on employees, customers, neighbours, etc; *guidelines* = rules or instructions on how to so something; *uphold* = make sure that something is obeyed
Paragraphs 8 and 9: 1. violating   2. terminate   3. concerns   4. redress   5. comply with   6. penalise   7. repercussions   8. responsibilities

Court orders and injunctions (page 23)

Note that many of the explanations of the orders and injunctions in this exercise define only one or two of their main features.

1. banning   2. ASBO (= *Anti-Social Behaviour Order*)   3. search   4. undertaking   5. interlocutory   6. restraining
7. friend   8. freezing   9. publication   10. non-molestation   11. occupation   12. Housing   13. Common
14. Restitution   15. discharge   16. penal   17. arrest   18. committal

Court structures (page 24)

1. The United Kingdom
1. Court of Justice of the European Communities   2. House of Lords   3. Court of Appeal (Criminal division)   4. Court of Appeal (Civil division)   5. Crown Court   6. High Court   7. Magistrates' Court   8. County Court

2. The USA
1. Supreme Court   2. Courts of Appeal (12 Circuits)   3. Court of Appeal (Federal Circuit)   4. Court of Military Appeals
5. 94 District Courts   6. Tax Court   7. Courts of Military Review   8. International Trade Court   9. Claims Court
10. Court of Veterans' Appeals

Crime 1: Categories (page 25)

Crimes against the person: abduction;   actual bodily harm;   assault;   battery;   grievous bodily harm;   indecent assault;   infanticide;   manslaughter;   murder;   paedophilia (also called *unlawful* sex);   racial abuse;   rape;   wounding. Note that some crimes against the person, such as murder and paedophilia, are also considered to be crimes against society
Crimes against property: arson;   being equipped to steal;   blackmail;   breaking and entering;   burglary (if the *burglar* is *armed*, this is called *aggravated burglary*);   criminal damage;   deception or fraud;   embezzlement;   forgery;   handling stolen goods;   money laundering;   piracy (specifically *intellectual property*. Note that *piracy* can also refer to the attacking of ships at sea in order to commit a robbery);   possessing something with intent to damage or destroy property;   robbery (if the *robber* is *armed*, this is called *armed robbery*);   theft
Public order offences: committing a breach of the peace;   drug dealing (the moving of drugs from one country to another is called *drug trafficking*);   misuse of drugs;   obscenity;   obstruction of the police;   possessing weapons;   unlawful assembly
Road traffic offences: careless or reckless driving;   driving without a licence or insurance;   drunk in charge
Sexual offences: bigamy;   indecency;   paedophilia;   rape
Political offences: breach of the Official Secrets Act;   bribery (especially if the person being bribed is a Member of Parliament);   espionage;   sedition;   terrorism;   treason
Offences against justice: aiding and abetting an offender;   bribery (especially if the person being bribed is, for example, a police officer or a juror);   conspiracy;   contempt of court;   perjury;   perverting the course of justice

Suicide, or *attempted suicide*, is not a crime, although it *is* a crime to help someone kill themselves, even in cases of *euthanasia* (*mercy killings*).

Note that the word *crime* can refer to one or more specific act ('*There has been a 50% rise in crimes of violence*') or it can refer to illegal acts in general ('*There has been a 50% rise in violent crime*').

Crime 2: Name the offence (pages 26 – 27)

1. arson   2. murder (or *attempted murder*, if the victim survived)   3. careless or reckless driving (specifically, *speeding*)
4. breaking and entering / burglary / theft (not *robbery*, as the crime took place in a private residence)   5. bribery
6. obscenity   7. aiding and abetting an offender   8. terrorism / wounding   9. (video) piracy   10. espionage (if the country is at war, the minister might also be accused of *treason*)   11. sedition (he might also be committing a *breach of the peace* at an *unlawful assembly*, and his address to the crowd might result in *vandalism* and *hooliganism*)   12. forgery (the bank note the customer is trying to use has been *forged*)   13. manslaughter (specifically *corporate manslaughter*)
14. deception or fraud (the man who went to the woman's house pretended to be someone he wasn't: he *deceived* her) / theft   15. abduction (we can also say *kidnapping*)   16.criminal damage   17. blackmail   18. perjury (the defendant is *perjuring himself* in court)   19. contempt of court   20. embezzlement   21. breach of the Official Secrets Act (= an Act of the British Parliament which governs the publication of secret information relating to the state)   22. (public) indecency (specifically *indecent exposure*)   23. perverting the course of justice   24. money laundering

For reference see *Dictionary of Law* 4th edition (A & C Black 0-7475-6636-4).

Answers (cont.)

Here are the sentences with the correctly-rearranged words and expressions:

1. Once the crime has been **committed**, it is **reported** to the police by the **victim**.
2. The police arrive at the **scene** of the crime to **investigate** what has happened.
3. They look for important **clues** and other **evidence** (for example, fingerprints or a genetic profile) that will help them to identify the **culprit**.
4. In some cases, they will also try to establish if the *modus operandi* (a Latin expression which describes the way in which the crime was carried out) matches other crimes in the area.
5. If they have a **suspect** who doesn't have a good **alibi**, they will then **apprehend** him.
6. When he is **arrested**, the police will **caution** him (in other words, they warn him that anything he says might be used later in court).
7. He is then taken to the police station, where he is **interviewed*** by the **investigating officers**.
8. He is allowed to have a **solicitor** present if he wants.
9. If he wants **legal representation** at this stage, but cannot afford it, the police must provide it.
10. If, at the end of the interview, the police believe that they have the right man, they **charge** him with the crime.
11. A **statement** is prepared, which is signed by all parties present.
12. The **accused** is then either **released** on **bail** (in other words, he is allowed to leave the police station and go home in exchange for a financial 'deposit', on condition that he promises to appear in court when required: if he doesn't appear in court, he will lose this deposit and a **warrant** will be issued for his **arrest**), or he is **remanded** in **custody**** and locked in a cell to prevent him from running away.
13. More questioning will probably follow: the police need as much **proof** as possible (anything that is **admissible** in court will help them to get a **conviction**), and they may also be interested in any **accomplices** who may have helped their man.
14. The police will also want to talk to any **witnesses** who were present when the crime took place.
15. The next day, the man appears before a **magistrate** in a **magistrates'** court. If the police present their **case** properly and have followed all the correct procedures and protocols, he will then be **committed** for **trial** at a **Crown** Court.

* We can also use *interrogated* or *questioned*. In Britain, the euphemistic expression '*helping the police with their enquiries*' is also used.
** We can also say *detained*.

Dispute resolution (page 31)

1. alternative 2. litigation (the verb is to *litigate*, the adjective is *litigious*) 3. voluntary / consent 4. impartial / mediator (the verb is *to mediate*) 5. facilitator 6. joint session / caucus 7. confidential/ disclosed 8. resolutions / practical / beneficial 9. negotiations 10. settlements / compromise / mutual 11. bound 12. prejudice 13. binding / honour / contractually 14. arbitration 15. tribunal 16. arbitrator 17. adjudication 18. public domain

Employment and human resources (pages 32 – 33)

1. employees 2. payroll 3. part-time (an employee who works part-time is a *part-timer*) 4. full-time (an employee who works full-time is a *full-timer*) 5. contract 6. duties *and / or* responsibilities 7. minimum wage 8. equal-opportunities 9. employer 10. dismiss (the noun is *dismissal*) 11. entitled 12. redundancy 13. alternative 14. health and safety 15. regulations 16. protection 17. industrial accidents 18. liable (the noun is *liability*) 19. injuries (the verb is *to injure*) 20. disabilities 21. compensation (the verb is *to compensate*) 22. monetary 23. negligence (the verb is *to neglect*) 24. dependant (the adjective is *dependent*) 25. compelled 26. (employment) tribunal 27. exceeds 28. consecutive 29. leave (this can be *paid* or *unpaid*) 30. pregnant (the noun is *pregnancy*) 31. childbirth 32. maternity leave (the period when a woman continues to receive payment is called the *maternity pay period*, or *MPP*) 33. maternity pay (also called *statutory maternity pay*, or *SMP*) 34. contributions (the verb is *to contribute*) 35. notice 36. ante-natal (we can also say *prenatal*. *Postnatal* refers to the period <u>after</u> giving birth) 37. suspend 38. paternity leave 39. parental 40. Discrimination 41. harassment / intimidation /bullying 42. grievance 43. allegation 44. grievance procedure

European courts, institutions and conventions (pages 34 – 35)
Here are the texts with the wrong words highlighted and corrected.

The European Union (EU)
This is a group of European **nations** that form a single **economic** community and have agreed on **social** and political cooperation. There are currently 25 member states. The Union has a **Parliament** and a main **executive** body called the European Commission (which is made up of members **nominated** by each member state).

The Council of Europe
This is one of the four bodies which form the basis of the European Union. The Council does not have fixed members, but the member states are each represented by the relevant **government** minister. The Council is headed by a President, and the **Presidency** rotates among the member states in alphabetical order, each serving a six-month period. This means that in effect each member can control the **agenda** of the Council, and therefore that of the European Union during their six-month period, and can try to get as many of its **proposals** put into **legislation** as it can.

The European Convention on Human Rights
This is a convention signed by all members of the Council of Europe covering the rights and **fundamental** freedoms of all its citizens, and aims to prevent **violations** and **breaches** of human rights. The convention recognises property rights, the right of citizens to **privacy**, the due **process** of law and the **principle** of legal review or **appeal**. The key provisions are now incorporated by the Human Rights Act of 1998, which came **into** force in the United Kingdom in October 2000.

The European Court of Human Rights
This is a court that considers the rights of citizens of states which are **parties** to the European Convention for the **protection** of human rights, and has **jurisdiction** over cases that cannot be **settled** by the European Commission of

For reference see *Dictionary of Law* 4th edition (A & C Black 0-7475-6636-4).

Human Rights (see below). It protects many **basic** rights, including the right to life, freedom from fear, freedom from torture, freedom of **speech**, freedom of **religious** worship, freedom of **assembly** and **association**, etc (in fact, most of the articles in the *Universal Declaration of Human Rights*, on which the European Convention is based: see the section on Human Rights on pages 44 – 48). Its formal name is the European Court for the Protection of Human Rights.

The European Commission of Human Rights
This is a body which **investigates** any breaches and **abuses** of the European Convention on Human Rights. It attempts to end **grievances**, especially if they **contravene** the articles detailed in the European Convention, and to help **aggrieved** parties reach a settlement without recourse to the European Court of Human Rights (see above).

The European Court of Justice (the ECJ)
This is a court set up to see that the principles of law as laid out in the Treaty of Rome are observed and **applied** correctly in the European Union, and has **jurisdiction** over issues of European Law. Its full name is the *Court of Justice of the European Communities*. The Court is responsible for settling **disputes** relating to European Union law, and also acting as a last Court of Appeal against **judgements** in individual member states.

Court judges in the ECJ are **appointed** by the governments of the member states for a period of six years. These judges come from all the member states, and bring with them the **legal** traditions of each state. The court can either meet as a full court, or in **chambers** where only two or three judges are present. The court normally conducts its business in French, although if an **action** is brought before the court by or against a member state, the member state can choose the language in which the case will be heard. The court can hear actions against **institutions**, or actions brought either by the Commission or by a member state against another member state. The court also acts as Court of Appeal for appeals from the Court of First Instance (CFI). The court also interprets legislation and as such acts in a semi-**legislative** capacity.

The family 1: Relationships (pages 36 – 37)

1. (c)   2. spouse   3. False. Generally a partner is someone you live with (and with whom you have a sexual relationship), although some people *do* refer to their spouse as their partner   4. No. Same-sex partners can get married in some countries, but will not be legally recognised as being married in Britain. However, from December 2005 Britain introduced Civil Partnerships, which give same-sex couples many of the same rights and responsibilities as married couples.   5. A *separation* (from the verb to *separate*) is the state of two married people no longer living with each other. A *divorce* is the legal termination of a marriage (*divorce* can also be a verb: to *divorce*)   6. annulled (the noun is *annulment*, the adjective is *annullable*)   7. bigamy   8. Usually (d) (if divorce proceedings are *defended*, they may be transferred to the High Court, but this is unusual: most divorce cases are now conducted by what is called the '*special procedure*', which means that couples do not need to go through a full trial. In London, divorce proceedings are dealt with by a special court called the *Divorce Registry*)   9. (3) adultery, (4) unreasonable behaviour (for example, *emotional cruelty, domestic violence*, etc), (5) desertion (most divorces are granted on conditions (3) and (4))

10.
Here is the complete text:

A request (the **petition**) is made by the **Petitioner** (= *the person applying for the divorce*) to the court for a divorce, in which the facts about the people involved and the reasons for the divorce are explained.
The court sends the divorce **petition** to the **Respondent** (= *the other spouse*), together with a form called an *Acknowledgement of Service* form, which he / she completes. In it, he / she indicates whether or not he / she wishes to **dispute** the divorce.
He / She returns this to the court within 7 days. (If he / she wants to **dispute** the divorce and / or its terms, he / she is sent another form to complete).
Assuming that the **Respondent** does not want to **dispute** the divorce or the terms, a copy of the Acknowledgement of Service form is sent to the **Petitioner**, who confirms the facts sent in their original **petition** by swearing an **affidavit**.
The court pronounces the **decree nisi**, an order ending the marriage subject to a full **decree absolute**, which comes later and ends the marriage completely.

11. support *or* maintenance   12. Probably yes. The marital status of the couple at the time the children were born does not affect this   13. Child Support Agency   14. Money is automatically removed from that partner's wages or salary before he / she receives it   15. (c)   16. (a) (it can also occasionally be applied to a wife who is ordered to support her divorced husband. If the couple were *not* married, one of them may be ordered to pay the other *palimony*)   17. (b), assuming they are not related (this does not apply if they have bought a house or property together and are considered *beneficial joint tenants*)   18. The person or persons most closely related to you. If you are married, for example, your next of kin is usually your husband or wife.

The family 2: Children (pages 38 – 39)

Exercise 1:
Here is the completed text:

A child can be defined as 'a person under the age of 18'. We can also use the word '**minor**'. The state of being less than 18 years old is called '**minority**'. When a child becomes 18, he / she reaches the age of **majority** and so is legally regarded as an **adult**. In other words, he/ she becomes **responsible** for his / her own actions, can sue, be sued or undertake **business** transactions.

In Great Britain a child does not have full **legal status** until the age of 18. A contract is not **binding** on a child, and a child cannot own **land**, cannot make a **will**, cannot **vote** and cannot drive a car (under the age of seventeen). A child cannot **marry** before the age of 16, and can only do so between the ages of 16 and 18 with the **written permission** of his / her **parents** or legal **guardians**. A child who is less than 10 years old is not considered capable of committing a crime; a child between 10 and 14 years of age may be considered capable of doing so if there is evidence of **malice** or knowledge, and so children of these ages can in certain circumstances be **convicted**. In criminal law the term 'child' is used for children between the ages of 10 and 14; for children between 14 and 17, the term '**young person**' is used; all children are termed '**juveniles**'. If someone between these ages commits a crime, he / she is known as a **young offender**, and may be sentenced in a **Youth** Court (previously known as a **Juvenile** Court).

For reference see *Dictionary of Law* 4th edition (A & C Black 0-7475-6636-4).

Answers *(cont.)*

Exercise 2:
1. benefit (*Support* is money paid regularly by one parent to the other parent, who is looking after a child / children. *Maintenance* is payment made by a divorced or separated husband or wife to the former spouse, to help pay for living expenses and also for the cost of bringing up the children. A *pension* is money a person receives when they retire)   2. False: it is called *access*   3. False: this is now done by the *Child Support Agency (CSA)*, an agency of the *Department for Work and Pensions: See The Family 1: Relationships on page 40*)   4. Acting in the place of a parent, with parental responsibilities (for example, while a child is at school, his / her teacher is *in loco parentis*)   5. delinquent (sometimes called a *juvenile delinquent*. The act of causing *delinquent* acts is called *delinquency*)   6. (b). (a) is called *fostering*. (c) is called *supervision* (usually as a result of a *supervision order*)   7. In theory, any of them, although married couples are generally preferred.
8. neglect / abuse   9. surrogate (if a man is unable to father a child, the couple may use a *surrogate father*. In both circumstances, the child is usually conceived through *artificial insemination*)   10. (c)   11. True: they can be liable for *negligence* and *damages* if they have given their children something 'dangerous' and which the children have failed to use responsibly. The same applies if the parents have not exercised sufficient parental control for a child of any particular age
12. True   13. This is when children deliberately stay away from school without their parents' or teachers' permission (a child who does this is called a *truant*. The verb is *to play truant* (*to play hooky* in the USA). Truancy is such a big problem in some cities that police have a special *truancy squad* to deal with it. Parents can be fined or sent to prison if their children play truant persistently)   14. 1 (h), 2 (f), 3 (d), 4 (g), 5 (c), 6 (a), 7 (e), 8 (b)

Human Rights 1 (pages 40 – 42)

Exercise 1:
1. equal   2. rights   3. conscience   4. entitled   5. distinction   6. race   7. political   8. jurisdictional   9. limitation
10. liberty   11. slavery   12. servitude   13. slave trade   14. prohibited   15. torture   16. degrading   17. discrimination
18. violation   19. incitement   20. tribunals   21. fundamental   22. constitution   23. arbitrary   24. detention   25. exile
26. impartial   27. obligations

Exercise 2:
Article 11: inocent = innocent,   trail = trial,   defense = defence,   comitted = committed,   penaltey = penalty
Article 12: arbitary = arbitrary,   privatecy = privacy,   reputeation = reputation,   projection = protection
Article 13: residents = residence,   boarders = borders,   estate = state
Article 14: assylum = asylum,   presecution = persecution (<u>not</u> *prosecution*),   inboked = invoked,   prossecutions = prosecutions,   principals = principles
Article 15: depraved = deprived,   denyed = denied
Article 16: limmitation = limitation,   religious = religion,   dissolluttion = dissolution,   consend = consent,   fondmental = fundamental
Article 17: asociattion = association,   abitrarily = arbitrarily
Article 18: consience = conscience,   believe = belief,   practise = practice (in British English *practise* is a <u>verb</u>, and we need a <u>noun</u> here),   warship = worship
Article 19: inteferance = interference,   frontears = frontiers
Article 20: asembly = assembly,   cambelled = compelled

Exercise 3:
Suggested answers (these are simplified versions of Articles 21 – 30):

Article 21: Everyone has the right to take part in their country's political affairs either by belonging to the government themselves or by choosing politicians who have the same ideas as them. Elections should take place regularly and voting should be in secret. Every adult should have the right to vote and all votes should be equal.
Article 22: The society in which you live should help you to develop and to make the most of all the advantages (culture, work, social welfare) which are offered to you.
Article 23: Every adult has the right to a job, and to receive a salary that can support him / her and his / her family. Men and women should get paid the same amount of money for doing the same job. Anyone can join a trade union.
Article 24: Everyone should have the right to rest from work and to take regular paid holidays.
Article 25: Everyone has the right to a good life, with enough food, clothing, housing and healthcare. You should be helped if you are out of work, if you are ill, if you are old or if your husband or wife is dead. Women who are going to have a baby should receive special help. All children should have the same rights, whether their mother is married or unmarried.
Article 26: Everyone has the right to go to school, and should go to school. Primary schooling should be free. Everyone should be able to learn a profession or continue their studies as far as possible. Everyone should be taught to get on with others from different races and backgrounds. Parents should have the right to choose how and what their children learn.
Article 27: Everyone should have the right to share in their community's arts and sciences. Works by artists, writers or scientists should be protected, and everyone should benefit from them.
Article 28: So that your rights are respected, there should be an 'order' to protect them. This 'order' should be both local and worldwide.
Article 29: Everyone should have duties towards their community and to other people. Human rights should be observed and protected by everyone in a spirit of mutual respect.
Article 30: Nobody should take away these rights and freedoms from us.

In Europe, there is also the *European Convention of Human Rights*. This is a convention signed by all members of the Council of Europe covering the rights of all its citizens. The key provisions are now covered by the *Human Rights Act of 1998* (which came into force in the United Kingdom in 2000, although it does not form part of English law). The Convention recognises property rights, religious rights, the right of citizens to privacy, the due process of law and the principle of legal review.

Human rights 2 (pages 43 – 44)

Note that some of these are open to debate and interpretation, and you may not agree with all of them. Some other circumstances may also be involved in each situation which are not mentioned. For the complete and original Universal Declaration of Human Rights, visit *www.unhchr.ch/udhr*.

1. Article 26   2. Article 8   3. Article 10   4. Article 24   5. Article 16   6. Article 20   7. Article 11, and probably Article 12

72

For reference see *Dictionary of Law* 4th edition (A & C Black 0-7475-6636-4).

8. Articles 6 and 7 (and probably also Article 3)   9. Articles 9, 13, 15, 19   10. Article 13   11. Article 7   12. Article 17
13. Article 14   14. Article 21   15. Article 19, and probably Articles 3, 5 and 9   16. Article 12   17. Articles 19 and 20
18. Article 12   19. Articles 12 and 19   20. Article 16   21. Articles 20 and 23   22. Articles 22 and 25   23. Articles 3, 5
and 11   24. Article 9, and probably also Article 3   25. Article 5   26. Articles 3 and 4   27. Article 18   28. Article 13
29. Article 23

Legal Latin (page 45)

1. ipso jure   2. in flagrante delicto   3. prima facie (for example, *There is a prima facie case to answer, so we will proceed with the case*)   4. ex gratia (for example, an *ex gratia payment*)   5. de novo   6. per se (for example, *His claim that he was confused at the time of his actions does not stand as a defence per se*)   7. locus standi (for example, *The taxpayer does not have locus standi in this court*)   8. inter alia (for example, *She demands possession of the house and custody of the children inter alia*)   9. ex parte (for example, *The wife applied ex parte for an ouster order against her husband*. The expression *without notice* is now usually used instead)   10. ex post facto   11. pari passu (for example, *The new shares will rank pari passu with the existing ones*)   12. mala in se   13. in terrorem   14. habeas corpus   15. de facto (for example, *He is the de facto owner of the property*)   16. pro tempore (for example, *We are prepared to issue a pro tempore injunction until the case is dealt with fully in the court*)   17. in personam (for example, *an action in personam*)   18. ipso facto (for example, *He was found in the vehicle at the time of the accident and ipso facto was deemed to be in charge of it*)   19. in loco parentis (for example, *The court is acting in loco parentis*)   20. res judicata   21. per curiam   22. doli capax   23. onus probandi (we can also say *burden of proof*)   24. uberrimae fidei (for example, an insurance contract is *uberrimae fidei*)   25. consensus ad idem   26. de jure (for example, *He is the de jure owner of the property*)   27. ad litem   28. non compos mentis (this can be a mitigating circumstance if a crime is committed)   29. bona vacantia (for example, in the case of a person without living relatives, dying without making a will: his / her property usually passes to the state)   30. mens rea (Generally, in order to be convicted of a crime, the accused must be shown to have committed an unlawful act (*actus reus*) with a criminal state of mind (*mens rea*))   31. quid pro quo   32. ab initio   33. in rem   34. actus reus   35. doli incapax (for example, children under the age of 10 are *doli incapax* and cannot be prosecuted for criminal offences; children between 10 and 14 are presumed to be doli incapax but the presumption can be reversed if there is evidence of knowledge or *malice*)   36. corpus delicti   37. mala prohibita (for example, walking on the grass in a park where this is not allowed. Compare *mala prohibita* with *mala in se*)   38. bona fide (for example: *The respondent was not acting bona fides*; *She made me a bona fide offer*)   39. ultra vires (for example, *The police were accused of acting ultra vires*)

Legal referencing (page 46)

1. thereinafter   2. thereinbefore   3. hereto   4. hereunder   5. herein   6. hereof   7. hereafter   8. hereto   9. therein
10. thereafter   11. heretofore   12. herewith   13. hereinafter   14. hereby   15. aforementioned

On the road (page 47)

1. reckless (for example, *tailgating*, *speeding*, etc. A driver who causes death through reckless or dangerous driving is guilty of a *notifiable offence* and may be charged with *manslaughter* or *culpable homicide*)   2. contravention (for example, a driver may be charged with a *contravention of speed limits*, a *contravention of parking regulations*, etc. The word *contravention* can be applied to *any* situation where a rule or regulation is broken)   3. speeding (we also say *exceeding the speed limit*)   4. joy riding (sometimes written as one word, *joyriding*. If someone breaks into a vehicle to steal it, this may be referred to as *aggravated theft*)   5. third party (third party insurance pays compensation if someone who is not the insured party incurs loss or injury. If the insured person is also covered, this is called *comprehensive* or *fully-comprehensive* insurance. In Britain, driving without third party insurance is an offence which can carry a fine of up to £5,000, and a possible *ban* from driving. The adjective is *uninsured*)   6. disqualified (if a driver in Britain commits a motoring offence, he / she receives *points* on his / her driving licence. If 12 or more points are accumulated over a three-year period, the driver is disqualified. Some offences carry more points than others)   7. fixed penalty (a set of fines and penalties established in advance, usually for minor motoring offences)   8. comply (for example, drivers should comply with traffic lights and signs, they should comply with the direction of a *traffic warden*, they should comply with *pedestrian crossing* regulations, etc)   9. defective   10. drink driving (in Britain, this automatically carries a ban from driving of at least one year, unless the driver has *mitigating circumstances*, or if a ban from driving would cause the driver exceptional hardship – for example, the loss of his / her job)   11. seatbelt (this rule includes front- and back-seat passengers)

Other driving offences in Britain include: driving while disqualified; driving without road tax; using a hand-held mobile phone while driving; failing to stop after an accident; failing to report an accident within 24 hours; driving with too many people in a vehicle, or with an otherwise overloaded vehicle; failing to supply police with an alcohol, blood or urine specimen when asked; driving while unfit through drugs; driving while failing to notify a disability; leaving a vehicle in a dangerous place, etc. There are, in fact, at least 60 offences you may commit by driving a motorised vehicle in Britain!

The word in the shaded vertical strip is *endorsement* (from the verb to *endorse*, definition 3 in the A & C Black *Dictionary of Law*)

People in the law 1 (pages 48 – 49)

Across: 2. lawyer   6. attorney (used especially in the USA)   11. juror   12. judiciary   13. advocate   15. testator (a woman who makes a will is called a *testatrix*)   16. barrister*   19. appellant   20. convict (we also say *prisoner*. *Convict* can also be a verb: *to convict* someone of a crime)   21. foreman (called the *foreman of the jury*)   23. probation (somebody who has been put *on probation* is called a *probationer*)   24. suspect (this can also be a verb: *to suspect* someone of something)   26. witness (this can also be a verb: *to witness* something)   27. judge* (this can also be a verb: *to judge* someone)

Down: 1. client   3. claimant (we can also say *litigant*. *Claimant* has replaced the word *plaintiff*)   4. jury*   5. beneficiary (someone who gives money, property, etc, to others in a will is called a *benefactor*)   7. magistrate* (also called a *Justice of the Peace*, or *JP* for short)   8. adjudicator (*arbitrator* has a similar meaning)   9. tortfeasor   10. prosecutor   14. defendant (also called *the accused* in criminal cases)   17. applicant   18. solicitor   22. coroner   25. counsel (for example, *defence counsel*, or *counsel for the prosecution*)

* For more information on barristers, magistrates, judges and juries, see *People in the law 2* on page 50.

For reference see *Dictionary of Law* 4th edition (A & C Black 0-7475-6636-4).

Answers (cont.)

<u>People in the law 2 (page 50)</u>

Here are the completed texts:

<u>Barristers</u>: In England and Wales, a *barrister* is a member of one of the **Inns of Court** (= the four law societies in London to which lawyers are members); he or she has passed examinations and spent one year in **pupillage** (= training) before being **called to the bar** (= being fully accepted to practise law). Barristers have the **right of audience** in all courts in England and Wales: in other words, they have the right to speak, but they do not have that right **exclusively**.

<u>Magistrates</u>: *Magistrates* usually work in **Magistrates' Courts**. These courts hear cases of petty crime, **adoption**, **affiliation**, maintenance and violence in the home. The court can **commit** someone for **trial** or for **sentence** in a *Crown Court*. There are two main types of magistrates: *stipendiary* magistrates (qualified lawyers who usually sit alone); **lay** magistrates (unqualified, who sit as a **bench** of three and can only sit if there is a justices' **clerk** present to advise them).

<u>Judges</u>: In England, *judges* are **appointed** by the Lord Chancellor*. The minimum requirement is that one should be a barrister or **solicitor** of ten years' standing. The majority of judges are barristers, but they cannot **practise** as barristers. **Recorders** are practising barristers who act as judges on a part-time basis. The appointment of judges is not a **political** appointment, and judges remain in office unless they are found guilty of gross **misconduct**. Judges cannot be Members of **Parliament**. **

<u>The jury</u>: Juries are used in **criminal** cases, and in some civil actions, notably actions for **libel**. They are also used in some coroner's **inquests**. The role of the jury is to use common sense to decide if the **verdict** should be for or against the **accused**. Members of a jury (called **jurors**) normally have no knowledge of the law and follow the explanations given to them by the judge. Anyone whose name appears on the **electoral register** and who is between the ages of 18 and 70 is **eligible** for **jury service**. Judges, magistrates, barristers and solicitors are not eligible for jury service, nor are priests, people who are on bail, and people suffering from mental illness. People who are excused jury service include members of the armed forces, Members of Parliament and doctors. Potential jurors can be **challenged** if one of the parties to the case thinks they are or may be **biased**.

* The Lord Chancellor is the member of the British government and of the cabinet who is responsible for the administration of justice and the appointment of judges in England and Wales. At the time this book was published, the role of Lord Chancellor was to be abolished and his / her role assumed by the Secretary of State for Constitutional affairs.

** Note that in the USA, state judges can be appointed by the state governor or can be elected; in the federal courts and the Supreme Court, judges are appointed by the President, but the appointment has to be approved by Congress.

<u>Privacy and data protection (page 51)</u>

1. compliy = comply, practise = practice (*practise* is a verb), principals = principles   2. procceced = processed, acurrate = accurate, relavent = relevant, secureity = security   3. infermation = information, supject = subject, acess = access
4. agencys = agencies   5. procesed = processed, unjustifried = unjustified, damaging = damage, destress = distress
6. detales = details, markit = market, ideals = ideas   7. decisive = decision (decisive is the adjective), effect = affect (effect is a noun), present = prevent   8. unaccurate = inaccurate, ammended = amended   9. clam = claim, condensation = compensation   10. preceedings = proceedings, sollution = solution

<u>Property (pages 52 – 53)</u>

<u>Exercise 1</u>:
1. freehold   2. *leasehold* is property which is held for a fixed period of time on the basis of a lease, but *freehold* is property held for an unlimited time   3. True   4. tenant   5. a realtor   6. False: it is *conveyancing*   7. The title deeds show who owns the property: you will need them if there are any disputes over who owns it, or when you need to sell the house. If you buy a house with a mortgage, the mortgage lender holds the title deeds until you have repaid the money you owe
8. Probably a *fixed-rate mortgage*, as the interest you pay on the mortgage will not increase with the national rate (for a fixed period of time, at least)   9. foreclosure   10. (c) *Joint tenancy* means that the people who bought the house jointly own the entire property. Compare this with *tenants-in-common*, where each person owns a share in the property depending on how much each spent on it   11. (c)   12. She would be very unhappy: somebody else has offered a higher price for the house and the seller has accepted that offer   13. encumbrance   14. stamp duty

<u>Exercise 2</u>: Here is the completed text:
1. You make an **offer** on the **asking** price (the price that the seller is asking for the house), which is accepted by the seller.
2. You **appoint** a solicitor to help you make your purchase.
3. You solicitor receives **confirmation** of your accepted offer, and also any necessary details from the estate agent.
4. The seller's solicitor sends your solicitor a draft **contract**. This is checked to make sure there are no unusual **clauses**.
5. At the same time, the seller's solicitor sends your solicitor the seller's **title deed**. This is carefully checked for any restrictions that might apply to **ownership** of the property. At the same time, the seller should make your solicitor aware of any problems with the property (for example, **disputes** with his / her neighbours, any approved or unapproved **alterations** that he / she has made to the property, relevant information on **boundaries** adjoining other properties and public land, **covenants** or **preservation** orders that may restrict development of the property, whether you will need to get planning permission before making changes to the property, etc).
6. If the contract is approved, copies of it are prepared for **signing** by both you and the seller.
7. Before you do this, however, your solicitor should ask the local **authority** (for example, the local town council) to **disclose** any information it has on **plans** for the area around the property you are buying (for example, there may be plans to build an airport at the end of your back garden, or a motorway across your lawn at the front).
8. At the same time, you should ask for a **survey** of the property by a chartered **surveyor**. He / she will tell you if there are any problems with the property (for example, rising damp, dry rot, unsound **structural** features, etc).
9. If you are happy with everything, you now sign the contract: you are now legally **bound** to buy the property (you cannot pull out of the agreement, unless further checks by your solicitor produce unfavourable information that has been kept secret from you; for example, he / she may discover that the property details the seller has provided are not accurate).
10. Your solicitor arranges a **completion** date with the seller's solicitor – this is the date when you will take official **possession** of the property – and both you and the seller exchange contracts through your solicitors. Your title deeds are prepared.

For reference see *Dictionary of Law* 4th edition (A & C Black 0-7475-6636-4).

11. You pay your solicitor his **fees**, the money for the property (assuming you have already paid a **deposit** on the property, you will now need to pay the outstanding **balance**), the relevant **stamp** duty and Land **Registry** fees.
12. You get your copy of the deeds and the key to the front door. Congratulations, and welcome to your new home!

Punishments and penalties (pages 54 – 55)

1. punishable (for example, a *punishable* act, or a crime *punishable with imprisonment*) (Note: not *punishing*, which describes something that is exhausting and makes you tired) / penalise and penal (a *penal code* is a set of laws governing crime and its punishment. A *penal institution* is a place such as a prison where convicted criminals are kept) 2. punitive (= something that is intended to punish. We can also say *exemplary damages*. *Punitive* can also come before other words such as *action, measures, sanctions, restrictions, taxes, tariffs*, etc) 3. pronounced sentence (we can also say *passed sentence*. *Sentence* can be a noun or a verb) 4. a deterrent (for example, *a long prison sentence will act as a deterrent to other possible criminals*) 5. *Corporal punishment*: he / she is physically beaten with a stick or a whip. *Capital punishment*: he / she is judicially killed / *executed* (he / she has committed a *capital crime* and receives the *death penalty* or a *death sentence*)*
6. He may be given *a caution* or *a warning* by the police to slow down. Alternatively he might be *fined* (police often issue *on-the-spot fines*, which you have to pay immediately) and / or be given *points* on his licence (if you receive too many points within a certain time period, your licence will be temporarily withdrawn). 7. He will almost certainly be *banned / disqualified* from driving for at least a year, and will probably be fined. If he causes an accident as a result of being *drunk in charge* of a vehicle, he might also be sent to prison. 8. convicted / acquitted 9. A custodial sentence involves sending someone to prison. A suspended sentence is a sentence of *imprisonment* which a court orders shall not take effect unless the *offender* commits another crime. *Probation* is often a feature of a suspended sentence: the individual (the *probationer*) must behave in a certain way, under the supervision of a *probation officer*. 10. He is not allowed to go in that bar again, and might also be banned from other bars / public places in the area. 11. In Britain, an ASBO (pronounced as one word) is an *Antisocial Behaviour Order*. This is an order which is applied for by the police against any individual over the age of 10 years old who is causing someone distress, harm or harassment, in order to restrict their behaviour. If an ASBO is breached, the individual can expect to be punished. An ABC is an *Acceptable Behaviour Contract*. This is a formal written agreement which an individual signs to say he will not act in an antisocial manner in the future. 12. A young person (in Britain, normally someone under the age of 18) who has committed a crime (a remand centre is a special prison for young people who have been remanded in custody) 13. Life imprisonment (for crimes such as murder. Note that life imprisonment does not necessarily mean the offender spends his / her entire life in prison: in the United Kingdom, life imprisonment for murder lasts on average 10 years) 14. imprison (= to send someone to prison) 15. True 16. Six months: concurrent sentences take place at the same time as each other. 17. good behaviour 18. False. He / she is sentenced to do unpaid work in the local community (the abbreviation is *CSO*). 19. They will have to pay money to the other company: a bond is a document in which a company or individual promises to pay money if something happens (for example, if they breach a contract) 20. injunction (for example, *The Beckhams' lawyer applied for an injunction to stop the publisher from printing the book*) 21. compensation (the defendant would be ordered to pay *compensatory damages* to the injured party) 22. He would be unhappy: his assets (= his money and other belongings) have been *frozen*, which means that he cannot take them out of the country (also called a freezing *injunction*, and known until 1999 as a *Mareva injunction*).

* Corporal punishment was abolished in England, Scotland and Wales in 1948, and in Northern Ireland in 1968. Capital punishment for murder was abolished in the United Kingdom in 1965.

Types of court (pages 56 – 57)

Exercise 1:
1. small claims court 2. Court of Appeal (also called an Appeal Court) 3. court-martial (Note that the plural form is *courts-martial*. It can also be a verb, usually used in the passive: *to be court-martialled*) 4. courthouse 5. County Court (there are about 270 County Courts in England and Wales. They are presided over by either district judges or circuit judges. They deal mainly with claims regarding money, but also deal with family matters, bankruptcies and claims concerning land) 6. European Court of Human Rights (its formal name is the *European Court for the Protection of Human Rights*) 7. employment tribunal (formally known as an *industrial tribunal*. The panel hearing each case consists of a legally qualified chairperson and two independent *lay* (= not legally qualified) people who have experience of employment issues. Decisions need to be *enforced* by a separate application to the court. Appeals are made to an *Employment Appeal Tribunal*) 8. magistrates' court 9. coroner's court (an investigation in a coroner's court is called a *coroner's inquest*. A coroner's inquest also decides what happens when treasure or something valuable that has been secretly hidden or lost is suddenly rediscovered) 10. Crown Court 11. Lands Tribunal 12. Commercial Court 13. rent tribunal 14. High Court 15. European Court of Justice (*ECJ* for short. It is also called the *Court of Justice of the European Communities*) 16. Court of Protection 17. Admiralty Court 18. House of Lords

Exercise 2:
1. Admiralty Court (HMS = *Her / His Majesty's Ship*, an abbreviation that precedes the names of ships of the *Royal Navy*) 2. (in the first instance) County Court 3. coroner's court 4. Commercial Court 5. employment tribunal 6. Court of Protection 7. small claims court (if the amount was for less than £5,000), 8. rent tribunal 9. (probably) the High Court 10. court-martial

Wills (page 58)

1. testament 2. of sound mind / of age 3. dependants 4. deceased 5. intestate 6. probate 7. administrator 8. codicil 9. executor 10. benefactor / beneficiary 11. estate 12. inherit / inheritance 13. trust / trustee 14. power of attorney 15. living wills

Word association 1 (pages 59 – 60)

1. absolute 2. abuse 3. action 4. adverse 5. arbitration 6. breach 7. capital 8. certificate 9. civil 10. common 11. compensation 12. consumer 13. contract 14. court 15. criminal 16. customs 17. defence 18. drug 19. fraudulent 20. freedom 21. identity 22. implied 23. industrial 24. joint 25. judgement (also spelt *judgment*) 26. judicial 27. jury 28. letter 29. limited 30. net (also spelt *nett*)

For reference see *Dictionary of Law* 4th edition (A & C Black 0-7475-6636-4).

Answers *(cont.)*

Word association 2 (page 61)

Notice: notice of allocation, notice of appeal, notice of dishonour, notice of motion, notice of opposition, notice of service, notice to quit

Oath: to administer an oath, to be under oath, to take the oath, oath of allegiance

Offer: to be under, to be open to offers (note that offer is used in the plural here), to be open for sale, offer of amends, price offer, offer to buy, offer to quit, offer to sell

Official: official channels, official copy, official mediator, Official Receiver, official referee, official return, official secret, Official Solicitor (note the capital letters used for Official Receiver and Official Solicitor, as these are specific positions in the legal profession)

Open: open court, open account, open credit, open-ended, open hearing, open prison, open verdict

Patent: patent agent, patent defect, patent examiner, patent holder, patent number, patent office, patent pending, patent proprietor, patent rights, patent specification, to register a patent

Personal: personal action, personal allowances, personal assets, personal chattels, personal conduct, personal effects, personal estate, personal income, personal injury, personal property, personal representative

Police: police authority, police bail, police constable, police court, police detective, police force, police inquiries, police inspector, police investigation, police officer, police protection,

Power: power of advancement, power of appointment, power of attorney, power of search, power politics

Preliminary: preliminary discussion, preliminary hearing, preliminary inquiries, preliminary investigation, preliminary reference, preliminary ruling

Private: private client, private detective, private effects, private land, private law, private nuisance, private ownership, private property, private prosecution

Registered: registered company, registered land, registered office, registered trade mark, registered user

Right: right of abode, right of audience, right of establishment, right of re-entry, right of reply, right of silence, right of way, right to reside

Special: special agent, special constable, special damages, special deposits, special directions, special indorsement

Statement: to make a statement, to make a false statement, statement of affairs, statement(s) of case, statement of claim, statement of truth, statement of value

Word association 3 (pages 62 – 63)

1. contract 2. within 3. against 4. breaking 5. order 6. abiding 7. above 8. common 9. down 10. hands
11. commercial 12. enforcement 13. practise 14. common 15. property 16. Succession 17. reform 18. claim
19. proceedings 20. cost 21. executive 22. aid 23. tender 24. separation 25. status

Your completed crossword grid should look like this:

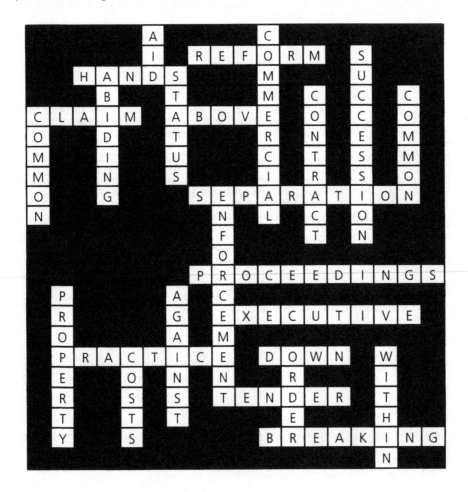

For reference see *Dictionary of Law* 4th edition (A & C Black 0-7475-6636-4).